BY THE SAME AUTHOR

POETRY
The Minotaur
Poems
RMS Titanic
Collected Poems 1950-1973
New and Selected Poems
41 Sonnet Poems 82
Reductionist Poem
Letter to an Englishman
The End of the Modern World
Relationships

NOVELS
The Life of Riley
Identity Papers

ESSAYS
A Question of Modernity
Heritage Now
An Irish Eye
Art for the People?

BIOGRAPHY
No Laughing Matter: The Life and Times of Flann O'Brien
Samuel Beckett: The Last Modernist

MEMOIRS
Dead as Doornails

Anthony Cronin was born in County Wexford. He is the author of several books of verse of which the most recent are *The Minotaur*, *Relationships* and *The End of the Modern World*. His prose books include *Dead as Doornails*, the novels, *Identity Papers* and *The Life of Riley* and biographies of Flann O'Brien and Samuel Beckett, as well as four collections of essays. He has edited and written for various journals, been cultural and artistic adviser to the Taoiseach and taught in the University of Montana and Drake University in the US. In 1983 he received the Marten Toonder award for his contribution to Irish literature.

ANTHONY CRONIN'S

Personal Anthology

Selections from his
Sunday Independent Feature

**NEW
ISLAND**

Anthony Cronin's Personal Anthology
First published December 2000
New Island Books
2 Brookside, Dundrum Road
Dublin 14

ISBN 1 874597 89 8

New Island gratefully acknowledges the generous assistance of the _Sunday Independent_ towards the publication of this volume.

British Library Cataloguing in Publication Data
A catalogue record for this book is available from the British Library

The Arts Council
An Chomhairle Ealaíon

New Island received financial assistance from The Arts Council (An Chomhairle Ealaíon), Dublin, Ireland.

Cover design: Slick Fish Design, Dublin
Cover painting by Michael Kane
Printed in Ireland by Colour Books, Dublin

Contents

Preface

Like the *Sunday Independent* piece of which it is a distill-
ation, this is a 'personal' anthology. It does not attempt to be
a selection of the 'best poems' of any particular place, period
or school, or even of 'good poems'. Here, simply, are poems
that I particularly like and, in some cases, have known and
loved for over half a century. When Aengus Fanning, the
Sunday Independent's remarkable editor, asked me if I would
like to select a poem a week for publication in the paper, he
made it clear that this was what he hoped they would be, and
that is what they are.

Of course I hope they are 'good poems'. Indeed I believe
some of them are a great deal more than that: dazzling,
moving, rewarding, sometimes overwhelming poems. And
some of them are quite humble, a quality which even an
overwhelming poem can easily possess.

Often, of course, my liking is only part of a more general
one – some of the poems here are among the best-known in
the language and have been much anthologised. But they are
here because I personally like them – which is not always the
case with well-known poems – and was glad to be able to
share that liking with others.

All the more surprising and pleasing then was the reader
response. In a fair number of years of writing journalism of
various kinds, I don't think I have ever had quite such a
reaction to a regular feature. And this provokes reflection.

The columns of a Sunday newspaper are, on the whole, a
fairly cheerful sort of context in which to come across poetry.
Other contexts in which we find it can be, by contrast, either
arcane or forbidding, sometimes deliberately so. 'AUTHOR-

ISED PERSONNEL ONLY' might be the sign hung over many such places.

And the familiars of these places have habits of discourse which many find intimidating. In both second and third level education poems are discussed in a way which makes many feel that they lack the equipment or the innate ability to respond. A poem is supposed to have a 'meaning' which can be paraphrased or re-stated. It is assumed there are beauties which only the properly trained reader can discern. These may be in the way of minute verbal effects invisible to the ordinary reader (perhaps intended to be invisible, or, sometimes, not intended at all); or they may take the form of ambiguities and subtleties which were overlooked by the reader until the critic got to work. And almost always there is a 'correct' way of responding to a poem of which the teacher or critic is aware but which the ordinary reader has to learn.

All this is, I think, a pity, and has resulted in a feeling among the ordinary reading public that there are difficulties about the appreciation of poetry which can not be overcome, even by effort. W. H. Auden's first book was published in 1930, when he was twenty-three. It brought him immediate fame in literary circles; but how little impact such 'fame' has on the general consciousness was demonstrated in extraordinary fashion when a poem of his, 'Funeral Blues' – not incidentally Auden's title – was included in a successful film, *Four Weddings and a Funeral*. Because there were no barriers, because the context was not forbiddiing or intimidating, Auden, whose work had been around for some sixty odd years, became for the first time a widely read poet.

Poetry is not something one should have to worry about; and it is certainly not something which should be confined to the ghettoes, where all the inhabitants seem to know each other and talk in a way that makes those who wander in off the busier streets feel like intruders.

And I don't believe one should bother too much about the meaning of a poem before it has sunk into the soul in other ways – through rhythm, sound and imagery. Accordingly I have tried to keep my prefatory notes as free from Eng. Lit. or Lit. Crit. in all their forms as possible. I may occasionally advert to what I think is the 'meaning' of a poem, what it is 'about', but I hope this is done without imposition. I have sought to get readers interested while keeping out of the way of their spontaneous response as much as I could. The poems in this book are meant to be enjoyed; though since I believe that poetry is the most enriching and exciting thing one can encounter in life, I do hope that having read and perhaps re-read them, readers will find themselves enriched.

In selecting poems for publication in a Sunday newspaper, considerations of length were important. Anything over forty lines was usually too long, and a high proportion of the poems I like are, of course, over forty lines. I have occasionally included extracts from longer poems – I could not resist the Goldsmith for example – but generally I have resisted the temptation. To set bounds to the painful issue of choice, I have excluded the living, young or old – though I did make an exception in the case of Francis Stuart when he was in his mid-nineties.

So, once again, my thanks to Aengus Fanning, not only for the original suggestion but for his encouragement through-out. And thanks too to other members of the *Sunday Independent* staff – to Ronan Farren, the literary editor, for his patience and tolerance; and Eamon Butler for all the work he put into checking copy and clearing copyright.

Anthony Cronin
Dublin, October 2000

With one or two obvious exceptions – W. B. Yeats, Robert Graves – poets found it increasingly difficult to write convincing love-poetry as the twentieth century wore on. Perhaps one of the reasons was that the love-poem is necessarily an affirmation and a pledge; and in our time the currency of affirmation and promise has been so seriously devalued by politicians, publicists and advertisers that it has become almost impossible to sound convincing.

Auden daringly avoids this difficulty by reminders of our human state. The lover admits to faithlessness; he knows that 'time and fevers' will burn away the beloved's beauty; that 'certainty, fidelity' will vanish on the stroke of midnight, and that 'every farthing of the cost' will have to be paid. But the lovers are nonetheless under a spell; and at least while the spell lasts everything is transformed.

Lullaby

by W. H. Auden

Lay your sleeping head, my love
Human on my faithless arm;
Time and fevers burn away
Individual beauty from
Thoughtful children, and the grave
Proves the child ephemeral:
But in my arms till break of day
Let the living creature lie,
Mortal, guilty, but to me
The entirely beautiful.

Soul and body have no bounds:
To lovers as they lie upon
Her tolerant enchanted slope
In their ordinary swoon,
Grave the vision Venus sends
Of supernatural sympathy,
Universal love and hope;
While an abstract insight wakes
Among the glaciers and the rocks
The hermit's sensual ecstasy.

Certainty, fidelity
On the stroke of midnight pass
Like vibrations of a bell,
And fashionable madmen raise
Their pedantic boring cry:
Every farthing of the cost,

All the dreaded cards foretell,
Shall be paid, but from this night
Not a whisper, not a thought,
Not a kiss nor look be lost.

Beauty, midnight, vision dies:
Let the winds of dawn that blow
Softly round your dreaming head
Such a day of sweetness show
Eve and knocking heart may bless,
Find the mortal world enough;
Noons of dryness see you fed
By the involuntary powers,
Nights of insult let you pass
Watched by every human love.

Matthew Arnold was something of a split personality. From being a dandified, elegant and ironic young man, who was very much 'the poet' in his manner and bearing, he grew into an over-conscientious public servant and voluminous commentator on the great issues of the Victorian era. The puritan conscience he had inherited from his father — the famous headmaster of Rugby School — triumphed, and instead of writing poetry he wrote books and articles about the German university system and the role of the state in middle-class education. 'Dover Beach' belongs to his second volume of verse, published in 1867. Though he was only forty-five, he wrote no more poems. His life is an object-lesson in high-minded time-wasting.

Dover Beach

by Matthew Arnold

The sea is calm tonight.
The tide is full, the moon lies fair
Upon the straits; — on the French coast the light
Gleams and is gone; the cliffs of England strand,
Glimmering and vast, out in the tranquil bay.
Come to the window, sweet is the night-air!
Only, from the long line of spray
Where the sea meets the moon-blanched land,
Listen! You hear the grating roar
Of pebbles which the waves draw back, and fling,
At their return, up on the high strand,
Begin, and cease, and then again begin,
With tremulous cadence slow, and bring
The eternal note of sadness in.

Sophocles long ago
Heard it on the Aegean, and it brought
Into his mind the turbid ebb and flow
Of human misery; we
Find also in the sound a thought,
Hearing it by this distant northern sea.

The Sea of Faith
Was once, too, at the full, and round earth's shore
Lay like the folds of a bright girdle furled.
But now I only hear
Its melancholy long, withdrawing roar,
Retreating, to the breath

Of the night-wind, down the vast edges drear
And naked shingles of the world.

Ah, love, let us to be true
To one another! For the world, which seems
To lie before us like a land of dreams,
So various, so beautiful, so new,
Hath really neither joy, nor love, not light,
Nor certitude, nor peace, nor help for pain;
And we are here as on a darkling plain
Swept with confused alarms of struggle and flight,
Where ignorant armies clash by night.

As a handsome but penniless – well, relatively penniless – young attaché at the British Embassy in Paris during the Second Empire, Wilfrid Scawen Blunt had a love-affair with one of the great courtesans of the time, Cora Pearl. The Esther poems, written late in life, reflect that experience.

Blunt went on to become a classically eccentric English gentleman. As an advocate of Egyptian, Irish and Indian freedom, he was a thorn in the side of the British establishment and served a brief sentence in Galway gaol during the land agitation.

Perhaps benefiting from Cora Pearl's teaching, he was also a noted amorist, numbering the young Lady Gregory among his innumerable conquests (in a tent, in the Egyptian desert, under the stars).

He was a convert to Islam and before he died in 1922, he was honoured by Yeats and Pound as a precursor of modernism in poetry.

With Esther

by Wilfrid Scawen Blunt

He who has once been happy is for aye
Out of destruction's reach. His fortune then
Holds nothing secret; and Eternity,
Which is a mystery to other men,
Has like a woman given him its joy.
Time is his conquest. Life, if it should fret,
Has paid him tribute. He can bear to die.
He who has once been happy! When I set
The world before me and survey its range,
Its mean ambitions, its scant fantasies,
The shreds of pleasure which for lack of change
Men wrap around them and call happiness,
The poor delights which are the tale and sum
Of the world's courage in its martyrdom;

When I hear laughter from a tavern door,
When I see crowds agape and in the rain
Watching on tiptoe and with stifled roar
To see a rocket fired or a bull slain,
When misers handle gold, when orators
Touch strong men's hearts with glory till they weep,
When cities deck their streets for barren wars
Which have laid waste their youth, and when I keep
Calmly the count of my own life and see
On what poor stuff my manhood's dreams were fed
Till I too learn'd what dole of vanity
Will serve a human soul for daily bread,

– Then I remember that I once was young
And lived with Esther the world's gods among.

John Betjeman sub-titled his second book, *Continual Dew*, '*a little book of bourgeois verse*'. It was published in 1937 and at that time those of the English bourgeoisie who were interested in poetry were waiting for the red dawn. The admired poets were the left-wingers, Spender and Cecil Day Lewis.

Betjeman used verse-forms and even rhyme-schemes which were more commonly used in light, or even comic, poetry. He wrote sympathetically of suburbs and garden cities and the Church of England and people who lived on the Southern Electric or the furthest reaches of the Bakerloo Line. When Auden expressed his admiration for these' bourgeois' verses, many were surprised.

What the critics missed were the underlying themes – mortality, loneliness, the futility of pretence and decorum when matched against the facts of life and death. Betjemen might uphold, as he said himself, essentially middle-class values. He might think that people who lived by rules and order were brave as well as superficial. But he is just as much a poet of the big themes of mortality and mutability as Yeats is.

What is the theme of 'Youth and Age on Beaulieu River, Hants'? Only pedants ask us to say what poems are 'about'. Probably the theme is just what the title says it is, youth and age. And all that they both bring with them in the way of loneliness and yearning, hope and knowledge, oddly but perfectly matched with the visual imagery and the jaunty but delicate rhythms.

Youth and Age on Beaulieu River, Hants

John Betjeman

Early sun on Beaulieu Water
Lights the undersides of oaks,
Clumps of leaves it floods and blanches,
All transparent glow the branches
Which the double sunlight soaks;
To her craft on Beaulieu water
Clemency the General's daughter
Pulls across with even strokes.

Schoolboy-sure she is this morning;
Soon her sharpie's rigg'd and free,
Cool beneath a garden awning
Mrs Fairclough, sipping tea
And raising large long-distance glasses
As the little sharpie passes,
Sighs our sailor girl to see;

Tulip figure, so appealing,
Oval face, so serious-eyed,
Tree roots passed and muddy beaches
On to huge and lake-like reaches
Soft and sun-warm, see her glide –
Slacks the slim young limbs revealing,
Sun-brown arm the tiller feeling –
With the wind and with the tide.

Evening light will bring the water,
Day-long sun will burst the bud,
Clemency, the General's daughter,
Will return upon the flood.
But the older woman only
Knows the ebb-tide leaves her lonely
With the shining fields of mud.

Asked to write 'an explication' of Robert Burns's great lyric, Richard Wilbur once said that, 'There is really no end to what need not be said about this poem.' He did, however, go on to point out that there is a shift between stanzas two and three, when the poem abandons the beloved and becomes a glorification of the poet's own emotion. This rejoicing in the emotion itself was, according to Wilbur, a characteristic of romantic love. Anyway, here it is, in all its breathtaking hyperbole and its disdain for the limitations of time and space.

A Red, Red Rose

by Robert Burns

O, my love's like a red, red rose
That's newly sprung in June;
O, my love's like the melodie
That's sweetly played in tune.

As fair art thou, my bonnie lass,
So deep in love am I;
And I will love thee still, my dear,
Til a' the seas gang dry.

Til a' the seas gang dry, my dear,
And the rocks melt wi' the sun;
And I will love thee still, my dear,
While the sands o' life shall run.

And fare thee weel, my only love!
And fare thee weel a while!
And I will come again, my love,
Tho' it were ten thousand mile.

All the Brontë sisters wrote poetry, and they published a book together at their own expense, which was well reviewed and sold two copies in the year after publication. In retrospect, though, it is clear that Emily, as one might guess from her novel, was the poet of the family. Together with Anne she invented an imaginary country called Gondal and many of her poems were supposed to have been written by Gondal's inhabitants. This starkly beautiful and more personal poem was written in 1843. The reference to death in the last line is not an idle one. In the previous year Aunt Elizabeth, who had looked after the children after the death of their mother, had died, as well as Patrick Brontë 's curate, William Weightman, and Charlotte's close friend, Martha Taylor. Death was a familiar despot in the Brontë household.

Moonlit Night

by Emily Brontë

How clear she shines! How quietly
I lie beneath her guardian light,
While heaven and earth are whispering me,
'Tomorrow, wake, but dream tonight'.
Yes, Fancy, come, my Fairy love!
These throbbing temples softly kiss;
And bend my lonely couch above
And bring me rest, and bring me bliss.

And this shall be my dream tonight;
I'll think the heaven of glorious spheres
Is rolling on its course of light
In endless bliss, through endless years;
I'll think there's not one world above,
Far as these straining eyes can see,
Where Wisdom ever laughed at Love,
Or Virtue crouched to Infamy.

Where, writhing 'neath the strokes of Fate,
The mangled wretch was forced to smile;
To match his patience 'gainst her hate,
His heart rebellious all the while.
Where Pleasure still will lead to wrong,
And helpless Reason warn in vain;
And Truth is weak and Treachery strong;
And Joy the surest path to Pain;

And Peace, the lethargy of Grief
And Hope, a phantom of the soul;
And Life, a labour, void and brief;
And Death, the despot of the whole!

Hart Crane was perhaps the only major 'modernist' who actually liked the modern world. Not for him Pound's mediaevalism or Eliot's disdain for democracy. He delighted in technical progress and he believed in the destiny of the democratic masses of the United States as fervently as Whitman had believed in it. The major work of his all-too-short career – cut short by suicide – is an epic poem, 'The Bridge', which begins with an evocation of the steel curves of Brooklyn Bridge.

In this beautiful passage from *The Bridge* he remembers the hoboes of his childhood, who rode the rods of the long transcontinental trains. It is a passage which, in a curious way, is central to American writing, looking back to Whitman and forward to the Beats. In this part of Crane's epic the Indian princess Pocohontas has come to symbolise the continent itself.

from The Bridge

by Hart Crane

                              Behind
My father's cannery works I used to see
Rail-squatters ranged in nomad raillery,
The ancient men – wifeless or runaway
Hobo-trekkers that forever search
An empire wilderness of freight and rails.
Each seemed a child, like me, on a loose perch,
Holding to childhood like some termless play.
John, Jake or Charley, hopping the slow freight
– Memphis to Tallahassee – riding the rods,
Blind fists of nothing, humpty-dumpty clods.

Yet they touched something like a key perhaps.
From pole to pole across the hills, the states
– They know a body under the wide rain;
Youngsters with eyes like fjords, old reprobates
With racetrack jargon – dotting immensity
They lurk across her, knowing her yonder breast
Snow-silvered, sumac-stained or smoky blue –
Is past the valley sleepers, south or west,
– As I have trod the rumorous midnights, too,

And past the circuit of the lamp's thin flame
(O Nights that brought me to her body bare!)
Have dreamed beyond the print that bound her name,
Trains sounding the long blizzards out – I heard
Wail into distances I knew were hers.
Papooses crying on the wind's long mane

Screamed redskin dynasties that fled the brain,
– Dead echoes! But I knew her body there,
Time like a serpent down her shoulder, dark
And space, an eaglet's wing, laid on her hair.

William Blake's poem used to be the anthem of the British Labour Party, sung along with 'The Red Flag' from party conference platforms; but, even though nobody knows quite what it means, it would probably be regarded as too radical for Tony Blair's New Labour.

I once heard William Empson expound on its meaning. From what he said I gathered that the 'dark satanic mills' were not the mills of the industrial revolution, but I cannot quite believe that.

The long, dreadfully obscure, prophetic poem, 'Milton', to which it forms a preface, seems to be in part an attack on the 'Hirelings of Court, Camp and University' and on the 'Fashionable fools' who 'depress the powers' of true painters by the 'prices they pretend to give for contemptible works or the expensive advertising boasts that they make of such works'. More power to William Blake's elbow, say I, while remarking that most of the radicalism of artists springs from some such roots.

'Jerusalem' is obviously about the kingdom of God on earth, an ancient dream. Was its inauguration ever part of British Labour Party policy?

Jerusalem

by William Blake

And did those feet in ancient time
Walk upon England's mountains green?
And was the holy Lamb of God
On England's pleasant pastures seen?

And did the Countenance Divine
Shine forth upon our clouded hills?
And was Jerusalem builded here
Among these dark Satanic Mills?

Bring me my Bow of burning gold:
Bring me my Arrows of desire:
Bring me my Spear. O clouds unfold!
Bring me my Chariot of fire.

I will not cease from Mental Fight,
Nor shall my Sword sleep in my hand
Till we have built Jerusalem
In England's green & pleasant Land.

This little poem was a sort of endpiece to a book of engravings, *For the Sexes: The Gates of Paradise*, that Blake, who was both painter and poet, published in 1793. In his recent book on Blake, Peter Ackroyd points out that he had also been doing illustrations for Edward Young's now largely (and unjustly) neglected *Night Thoughts*, which contains the line, 'Thy Master, Satan, I dare call a dunce'. For Blake, Satan was the god of the material world, of the scientist and the scholar as well as of the manufacturer and industrialist; and for the most part it was he who was worshipped, even under the names of Jesus and Jehovah. Commentators have written much about the 'meaning' of the lines, which at any rate contain one profound truth – we are always the same person no matter what our actions – but whatever Blake 'meant', the lines have great incantatory power.

To The Accuser Who Is The God of This World

by William Blake

Truly, my Satan, thou art but a Dunce,
And dost not know the Garment from the Man.
Every Harlot was a Virgin once,
Nor can'st thou ever change Kate into Nan.

Though thou art Worshipped by the Names Divine
Of Jesus and Jehovah, thou art still
The Son of Morn in weary Night's decline,
The lost Traveller's Dream under the Hill.

Roy Campbell is writing about Luis de Camoes or Camoens — either way it's three syllables — the great sixteenth-century Portuguese epic poet. Camoes' adventures included the loss of an eye in service against the Moors, imprisonment in Portugal, and shipwreck off the coast of China.

Campbell too led an adventurous life and, though he never suffered imprisonment, managed to make himself unpopular both in Britain and in his native South Africa. He fought on the Franco side in the Spanish Civil War when numbers of more fashionable poets were making propaganda for the Spanish government; and he attacked both the Bloomsbury literary establishment and its left-wing counterpart of the 1930s. He died in a car crash in Portugal in 1957.

His sonnet to Camoes, written while on active service in Africa during the Second World War, rises above the tortuous entanglements of both their lives while acknowledging a fellowship in misfortune.

It also affirms that the hope of finding an illumination of our own experience is one of the best reasons for reading anything; and it manages as well to make a definition of poetry, which is precisely a way of wrestling one's 'hardships into forms of beauty' and teaching one's 'gorgon destinies to sing'.

Luis de Camoes

by Roy Campbell

Camoes, alone, of all the lyric race,
Borne in the black aurora of disaster,
Can look a common soldier in the face:
I find a comrade where I sought a master:
For daily, while the stinking crocodiles
Glide from the mangroves on the swampy shore,
He shares my awning on the dhow, he smiles,
And tells me that he lived it all before.
Through fire and shipwreck, pestilence and loss,
Led by the ignis fatuous of duty
To a dog's death – yet of his sorrows king –
He shouldered high his voluntary Cross,
Wrestled his hardships into forms of beauty,
And taught his gorgon destinies to sing.

I first read Padraic Colum's poem when I was quite young. There were such old women then, lone beggarwomen who tramped from town to town and house to house in search of food and shelter; and the gap between what the poor old beggarwoman of the poem hoped for and what she was ever likely to have struck me with poignant force. It still does whenever I read it. The poem deals with a reality that Colum, who was a workhouse-keeper's son, knew well. I don't think it is at all sentimental. The little house, like a Dutch interior, is imagined with great passion and detail; and the poem still says something about want, homelessness and isolation — as well as about the need to own things — which are relevant to the human condition, even in this affluent age.

The Old Woman of The Roads

by Padraic Colum

Oh, to have a little house!
To own the hearth and stool and all!
The heaped-up sods upon the fire,
The pile of turf against the wall!

To have a clock with weights and chains
And pendulum swinging up and down,
A dresser filled with shining delph,
Speckled and white and blue and brown!

I could be busy all the day
Clearing and sweeping hearth and floor,
And fixing on their shelf again
My white and blue and speckled store!

I could be quiet there at night
Beside the fire and by myself,
Sure of a bed and loth to leave
The ticking clock and the shining delph!

Och! But I'm weary of mist and dark,
And roads where there's never a house or bush,
And tired I am of bog and road
And the crying wind and the lonesome hush!

And I am praying to God on high,
And I am praying Him night and day,
For a little house, a house of my own –
Out of the wind's and the rain's way.

John Cornford was a tragically young casualty of the Spanish Civil War, a poet of bright, unlimited promise who was only twenty-one when he was killed during the second battle of the Ebro. Before he died he sent this beautiful poem to his friend Margot Heinemann. Because it did happen, the poet's death, part of the irredeemable wastefulness of war, has become a sort of sub-text in the poem, adding immeasurably to its already great beauty and pathos.

To Margot Heinemann

by John Cornford

Heart of the heartless world,
Dear heart, the thought of you
Is the pain at my side,
The shadow that chills my view.

The wind rises in the evening,
Reminds that autumn is near.
I am afraid to lose you,
I am afraid of my fear.

On the last mile to Huesca,
The last fence for our pride,
Think so kindly, dear, that I
Sense you at my side.

And if bad luck should lay my strength
Into the shallow grave,
Remember all the good you can;
Don't forget my love.

Ernest Dowson was a member of what Yeats called 'the tragic generation', the symbolists and decadents who flourished – if that is the word – in the 1890s. The often sordid and miserable details of his own existence, the central fact of which was a hopeless love for a Soho café owner's daughter who married a waiter, play little part in a poetry full of vague regrets and sorrows, symbolically expressed but not particularised. Like Wilde, Beardsely, Francis Thompson and Lionel Johnson, he was converted to Catholicism. Like most of them, he did not survive long into the new century; but it was in this little poem that T. S. Eliot later claimed to have detected that 'slight but significant shift of rhythm' which heralded the poetry of a new age. Phrases and lines from Dowson's work have transferred into the popular consciousness, though few people are aware of where they come from.

Vitae Summa Brevis

by Ernest Dowson

They are not long, the weeping and the laughter,
Love and desire and hate:
I think they have no portion in us after
We pass the gate.

They are not long, the days of wine and roses:
Out of a misty dream
Our path emerges for a while, then closes
Within a dream.

Hartley Coleridge was the eldest son of Samuel Taylor Coleridge and he had all his father's difficulties without having equivalent genius. A gentle soul, who seemed to lack concentration and a capacity for sustained effort, he was an alcoholic and drank his way out of an Oxford fellowship and various schoolmastering jobs. He published only one collection, *Poems, Songs and Sonnets*; and he died in 1849, aged fifty-five.

Long Time A Child ...

by Hartley Coleridge

Long time a child, and still a child, when years
Had painted manhood on my cheek, was I –
For yet I lived like one not born to die;
A thriftless prodigal of smiles and tears,
No hope I needed, and I knew no fears.
But sleep, though sweet, is only sleep, and waking.
I waked to sleep no more, at once o'ertaking
The vanguard of my age, with all arrears
Of duty on my back, nor child, nor man,
Nor youth, nor sage, I find my head is grey,
For I have lost the race I never ran:
A rathe December blights my lagging May;
And still I am a child, tho' I be old,
Time is my debtor for my years untold.

Samuel Taylor Coleridge, drunkard, drug addict, plagiarist, dreamer and – some would say – political renegade, is one of the great casualties of the romantic movement, his name almost an immediate evocation of fruitless effort and failure of purpose. What is often forgotten, though, is the sheer volume of his writings, including a huge amount of political journalism; and his serious and agonising efforts to break his addiction to opium.

Our general picture of Coleridge is deeply affected by his own readiness to engage in often unjustified self-reproach. His poetry was ruined for generations of people by over-representation in the schoolbooks – *Kubla Khan* and *The Ancient Mariner* with their metaphysical overtones, are almost a complete turn-off for young minds – and his philosophical writings suffer nowadays from the cold chill that the word 'metaphysics' sends through the blood. *Work Without Hope* belongs to his (comparatively serene) later years.

Work Without Hope

by Samuel Taylor Coleridge

All Nature seems at work. Slugs leave their lair —
The bees are stirring — birds are on the wing —
And Winter, slumbering in the open air,
Wears on his smiling face a dream of Spring!
And I, the while, the sole unbusy thing,
Nor honey make, nor pair, nor build, nor sing.

Yet well I ken the banks where amaranths blow,
Have traced the fount whence streams of nectar flow,
Bloom, O ye amaranths! Bloom for whom ye may,
For me ye bloom not! Glide, rich streams, away!
With lips unbrightened, wreathless brow, I stroll:
And would you learn the spells that drowse my soul?
Work without Hope draws nectar in a sieve,
And Hope without an object cannot live.

Arthur Hugh Clough had a hard time of it from Lytton Strachey in *Great Victorians*, in which he was the ineffectual poet tying up endless parcels for the imperious Miss Florence Nightingale.

In fact he was quite a tough-minded fellow who resigned an Oxford Fellowship rather than subscribe to the doctrines of the Church of England and became, like his friend Matthew Arnold, a school inspector instead.

He was the classical agnostic, declaring that his creed was not to pretend to know about things of which no knowledge was possible. He published few poems in his lifetime; but among those published after his death was *Amours De Voyage*, an astonishingly modern and very funny novel-in-verse about English tourists in Rome. He was in fact a precursor of modernism who believed that 'poetry should deal more with general wants and ordinary feelings'.

The Latest Decalogue

by Arthur Hugh Clough

Thou shalt have one God only; who
Would be at the expense of two?
No graven images may be
Worshipped except the currency.
Swear not at all, for, for thy curse
Thine enemy is none the worse.
At church on Sunday to attend
Will serve to keep the world thy friend.
Honour thy parents, that is, all
From whom advancement may befall.
Thou shalt not kill, but needst not strive
Officiously to keep alive.
Do not adultery commit;
Advantage rarely comes of it.
Thou shalt not steal, an empty feat,
When it's so lucrative to cheat.
Bear not false witness, let the lie
Have time on its own wings to fly.
Thou shalt not covet, but tradition
Approves all forms of competition.

The sum of all is, thou shalt love,
If anybody, God above.
At any rate shall never labour
More than thyself to love thy neighbour.

John Davidson is usually referred to as an 1890s' figure; and at first sight his career bears strong resemblances to that of other poets of the era. He contributed to the 'Yellow Book'; he was a member of the Rhymer's Club; he had a talent for not getting on in the world; and in the end, like other figures of the decade, he committed suicide, walking into the sea off the Cornish coast.

There is something a good deal grittier and tougher about Davidson than about some of the others, however; and it is reflected in his poetry along with his interest in science and philosophy. Because – unlike some of the others – he had to earn his living, he wrote too much rather than too little, turning out novels, plays and essays as well as much journalism and some perhaps over-ambitious long poems.

from 'Snow'

by John Davidson

Who affirms that crystals are alive?
I affirm it, let who will deny:
Crystals are engendered, wax and thrive,
Wane and wither, I have seen them die.

Trust me, masters, crystals have their day,
Eager to attain the perfect norm,
Lit with purpose, potent to display
Facet, angle, colour, beauty, form.

Water-crystals need for flower and root
Sixty clear degrees, no less, no more;
Snow, so fickle, still in this acute
Angle thinks, and learns no other lore:

Such its life, and such its pleasure is,
Such its art and traffic, such its gain,
Evermore in new conjunctions this
Admirable angle to maintain.

Crystalcraft in every flower and flake
Snow exhibits, of the welkin free:
Crystalline are crystals for the sake,
All and singular, of crystalry.

Yet does every crystal of the snow
Individualize, a seedling sown

Broadcast, but instinct with power to grow
Beautiful in beauty of its own.

Every flake with all its prongs and dints
Burns ecstatic as a new-lit star:
Men are not more diverse, fingerprints
More dissimilar than snow-flakes are.

There is no doubt about the popularity of Walter De La Mare's *The Listeners*, which time and again reaches first place in surveys of favourite poems. Even its presence in generations of schoolbooks – so often a killer – does not seem to have dulled its effect, nor does constant reprinting seem to render it over-familiar to readers of anthologies. I must have re-read it hundreds of times since I first encountered it in a schoolbook and its effect has certainly not lessened.

The Listeners

by Walter De La Mare

'Is there anybody there?' said the Traveller,
Knocking on the moonlit door;
And his horse in the silence champed the grasses
Of the forest's ferny floor:
And a bird flew up out of the turret,
Above the Traveller's head:
And he smote upon the door again a second time;
'Is there anybody there?' he said.
But no-one descended to the Traveller;
No head from the leaf-fringed sill
Leaned over and looked into his grey eyes,
Where he stood perplexed and still.
But only a host of phantom listeners
That dwelt in the lone house then
Stood listening in the quiet of the moonlight
To that voice from the world of men:
Stood thronging the faint moonbeams on the dark stair,
That goes down to the empty hall,
Harkening in an air stirred and shaken
By the lonely Traveller's call.
And he felt in his heart their strangeness,
Their stillness answering his cry,
While his horse moved, cropping the dark turf,
'Neath the starred and leafy sky;
For he suddenly smote on the door, even
Louder, and lifted his head: —
'Tell them I came, and no-one answered,
That I kept my word', he said.

Never the least stir made the listeners,
Though every word he spake
Fell echoing through the shadowiness of the still house
From the one man left awake:
Ay, they heard his foot upon the stirrup,
And the sound of iron on stone,
And how the silence surged softly backward,
When the plunging hoofs were gone.

Walter De La Mare wrote several often-anthologised poems besides 'The Listeners'; but this is one which has had less frequent outings than some others. Its title suggests a song from a play, indeed a Shakespeare play; and like Shakes-peare's songs it melodiously uses nonsense associations; but it has no context, nor, in its heart-breaking beauty and obvious depth of feeling, does it need one.

The Song of the Mad Prince

by Walter De La Mare

Who said, 'Peacock Pie'?
The old King to the sparrow:
Who said, 'Crops are ripe'?
Rust to the harrow:
Who said, 'Where sleeps she now?
Where rests she now her head,
Bathed in eve's loveliness'?
That's what I said.

Who said, 'Ay, mum's the word'?
Sexton to willow:
Who said, 'Green dusk for dreams,
Moss for a pillow'?
Who said, 'All Time's delight
Hath she for narrow bed;
Life's troubled bubble broken'?
That's what I said.

Dowson's tendency to idealise his sometimes sordid situation and to cloak the perhaps squalid particular circumstance in poetic symbolism has been remarked on here before. In his autobiography Yeats tells us that when he first became acquainted with Dowson and his friends, he 'began to hear in some detail of the restaurant keeper's daughter, and of her marriage to the waiter, and of the weekly game of cards with her that filled so great a share of Dowson's emotional life. Sober, he would look at no other woman, it was said, but, drunk, desired whatever woman chance brought, clean or dirty.' As with the previous Dowson poem included here, phrases from this one have achieved a currency among song-writers and others who may never have heard of Ernest Dowson.

Cynara

by Ernest Dowson

Last night, ah, yesternight, betwixt her lips and mine
There fell thy shadow, Cynara! Thy breath was shed
Upon my soul between the kisses and the wine;
And I was desolate and sick of an old passion,
Yea, I was desolate and bowed my head:
I have been faithful to thee, Cynara! In my fashion.

All night upon mine heart I felt her warm heart beat,
Night-long within mine arms in love and sleep she lay;
Surely the kisses of her bought red mouth were sweet;
But I was desolate and sick of an old passion,
When I awoke and found the dawn was gray:
I have been faithful to thee, Cynara! In my fashion.

I have forgot much, Cynara! Gone with the wind,
Flung roses, roses riotously with the throng,
Dancing, to put thy pale, lost lilies out of mind;
But I was desolate and sick of an old passion,
Yea, all the time, because the dance was long:
I have been faithful to thee, Cynara! In my fashion.

I cried for madder music and for stronger wine,
But when the feast is finished and the lamps expire,
Then falls thy shadow, Cynara! The night is thine;
And I am desolate and sick of an old passion,
Yea, hungry for the lips of my desire:
I have been faithful to thee, Cynara! In my fashion.

I am indebted for this delightful little poem to the W. H. Auden and John Garret anthology, *The Poet's Tongue*, published in 1935; but I am afraid I know nothing about Colin Francis except that his birth date is given by Auden and Garrett as 1895. I have looked in various other anthologies and works of reference for his name without success and in fact I would be grateful for any information readers can supply.

Tony O

by Colin Francis

Over the bleak and barren snow
A voice there came a-calling;
'Where are you going to, Tony O!
Where are you going this morning?'

'I am going where there are rivers of wine,
The mountains bread and honey;
There kings and queens do mind the swine,
And the poor have all the money.'

In January 1700, John Dryden contributed a short masque, known as 'The Secular Masque', to a benefit performance arranged for him in a London theatre. Dryden was then in his seventieth year. During the old century he had seen no less than four major changes of regime in England and changed sides himself three times. This is the closing chorus of the masque. Within its brief compass, it alludes variously to the hunt, to what Sir Walter Scott called 'the licentious gallantry which prevailed in the court of Charles II' and to the civil wars which had racked England in the seventeenth century.

Chorus from The Secular Masque

by John Dryden

'Tis well an old age is out:
And time to begin a new.

All, all of a piece throughout:
Thy chase had a beast in view;
Thy wars brought nothing about;
Thy lovers were all untrue.

'Tis well an old age is out,
And time to begin a new.

John Hewitt was born in Belfast of what he liked to describe as 'planter' stock. He was a sober, thoughtful, formalistic and moral poet whose work is always grounded in some immediate reality, whether the landscape of Co. Antrim or the history of some particular locality. He was a museum curator by profession and this took him to Coventry in middle life. The oscillation of mood described in this particular poem will, I think, find an echo in the experience of many other exiles.

An Irishman In Coventry

by John Hewitt

A full year since, I took this eager city,
the tolerance that laced its blatant roar,
its famous steeples and its web of girders,
an image of the state hope argued for,
and scarcely flung a bitter thought behind me
on all that flaws the glory and the grace
which ribbons through the sick, guilt-clotted legend
of my creed-haunted, Godforsaken race.
My rhetoric swung round from steel's high promise
to the precision of the well-gauged tool,
tracing the logic in the vast glass headlands,
the clockwork horse, the comprehensive school.

Then, sudden, by occasion's chance concerted,
in enclave of my nation, but apart,
the jigging dances and the lilting fiddle
stirred the old rage and pity in my heart.
The faces and the voices blurring round me,
the strong hands long familiar with the spade,
the whiskey-tinctured breath, the pious buttons,
called up a people endlessly betrayed
by our own weakness, by the wrongs we suffered
in that long twilight over bog and glen,
by force, by famine and by glittering fables
which gave us martyrs when we needed men,
by faith which had no charity to offer,
by poisoned memory and by ready wit,

with poverty corroded into malice
to hit and run and howl when it is hit.

This is our fate: eight hundred years' disaster
crazily tangled as the *Book of Kells*,
the dream's distortion and the land's division,
the midnight raiders and the prison cells.
Yet like Lir's children banished to the waters
our hearts still listen for the landward bells.

Ben Jonson was, like his friend William Shakespeare, a professional actor and playwright. He led a more adventurous life than Shakespeare and saw military service in Flanders, where, as he used to boast in his cups, he had 'killed his man in the sight of both armies'. He also killed a fellow actor in a duel, a crime for which he escaped hanging, but was branded by the common hangman as a felon. In the winter of 1618 he made his way on foot to Scotland where he stayed with another poet, William Drummond, laird of Hawthornden. Drummond took notes of his fascinating conversation, including many derogatory remarks about Shakespeare and other contemporaries.

An Ode to Himself

by Ben Jonson

Where dost thou careless lie,
Buried in ease and sloth?
Knowledge that sleeps doth die;
And this security,
It is the common moth
That eats on wits and arts, and oft destroys them both.

Are all the Aonian springs
Dried up? Lies Thespia waste?
Doth Clarius' harp want strings,
That not a nymph now sings?
Or droop they as disgraced,
To see their seats and bowers by chattering pies defaced?

If hence thy silence be,
As 'tis too just a cause,
Let this thought quicken thee:
Minds that are great and free
Should not on fortune pause;
'Tis crown enough to virtue still, her own applause.

Then take in hand thy lyre;
Strike in thy proper strain;
With Japhet's line aspire
Sol's chariot for new fire
To give the world again;
Who aided him will thee, the issue of Jove's brain.

And, since our dainty age
Cannot endure reproof,
Make not thyself a page
To that strumpet the stage;
But sing high and aloof,
Safe from the wolf's black jaw, and the dull ass's hoof.

D. H. Lawrence achieved a world-wide reputation through his humourless, turgid and, to my mind, almost unreadable novels, of which one, *Lady Chatterly's Lover*, brought him great notoriety as well.

He is, I think, much better value as a poet; and his later poems are intoxicating expressions of his truly rebellious spirit. An early draft of this splendid ballad reads:

> In such a Cash-Chemist University, what can they teach
> but cash-chemistry, cash-physics, cash-classics and cash-
>   culture altogether?

This, of course, is now the case in all universities, at least in the sense that what is taught is intended to be converted into cash as effectively as possible by the recipient of the education.

Nottingham's New University

by D. H. Lawrence

In Nottingham, that dismal town
where I went to school and college,
they've built a new university
for a new dispensation of knowledge.

Built it most grand and cakeily
out of the noble loot
derived from shrewd cash-chemistry
by good Sir Jesse Boot.

Little I thought, when I was a lad
and turned my modest penny
over on Boot's Cash Chemist's counter,
that Jesse, by turning many

Millions of similar honest pence
over, would make a pile
that would rise at last and blossom out
in grand and cakey style

Into a university
where smart men would dispense
doses of smart cash chemistry
in language of common sense!

That future Nottingham lads would be
cash-chemically B.Sc.

That Nottingham lads would rise and say;
— By Boots I am M.A.

From this I learn, though I knew it before
that culture has her roots
in the deep dung of cash, and lore
is a last offshoot of Boots.

A busy man, who took a large part of the world on his shoulders, George Russell, 'AE', wrote very few poems in later years. This was almost his last and it emerged from a long silence. It is also, I think, by far his finest, so the moral for poets is plain: never quite give up.

Germinal

by George Russell

Call not thy wanders home as yet
  Though it be late.
Now is his first assailing of
  The invisible gate.
Be still through that light knocking. The hour
  Is thronged with fate.

To that first tapping at the invisible door
  Fate answereth.
What shining image or voice, what sigh
  Or honied breath,
Comes forth, shall be the master of life
  Even to death.

Satyrs may follow after. Seraphs
  On crystal wing
May blaze. But the delicate first comer
  It shall be king.
They shall obey, even the mightiest,
  That gentle thing.

All the strong powers of Dante were bowed
  To a child's mild eyes,
That wrought within him that travail
  From depths up to skies,
Inferno, Purgatoria
  And Paradise.

Amid the soul's grave councillors
  A petulant boy
Laughs under the laurels and purples, the elf
  Who snatched at his joy,
Ordering Caesar's legions to bring him
  The world for his toy.

In ancient shadows and twilights
  Where childhood had strayed,
The World's great sorrows were born
  And its heroes were made.
In the lost boyhood of Judas
  Christ was betrayed.

Let that young wanderer dream on;
  Call him not home.
A door opens, a breath, a voice
  From the ancient room,
Speaks to him now. Be it dark or bright
  He is knit with his doom.

Many English nursery rhymes go back to the seventeenth century. Scholars have attempted to prove that some — *Humpty Dumpty* for example — are coded references to political events of their time. Others are derived from street-cries, riddles, proverbs and children's games. Their lasting appeal is, however, because they seem to be pure poetry, serving no purpose whatever. And very good poetry too, as good as most of the poetry that the fortunate children who learn them will encounter in after life. Here are two of my own favourites.

Two Nursery Rhymes
Anon

Doctor Foster

Doctor Foster went to Gloucester
In a shower of rain.
He stepped in a puddle
Right up to his middle
And never went there again.

Bed-time

'Let's go to bed,' said Sleepy-head,
'Tarry a while,' said Slow.
'Put on the pan,' said greasy Nan,
'We'll sup before we go.'

George Herbert was one of the English 'metaphysicals', a group of early seventeenth century poets, some of them country clergymen, which also included John Donne. Jeered at by Samuel Johnson and other eighteenth century critics for their far-fetched metaphors and general obscurity, the metaphysicals went out of fashion; but were rediscovered in our own time through the advocacy of T. S. Eliot and the researches of Herbert Grierson. The most obscure thing in this poem seems to me to be the reference to 'Angel's age' in the first line; but like most obscurity it is best dealt with by passing on and enjoying the rest. Herbert died of consumption at forty and his poems were first published by his friends after his death.

Prayer

by George Herbert

Prayer, the Church's banquet, Angel's age.
God's breath in man returning to his birth,
The soul in paraphrase, heart in pilgrimage,
The Christian plummet sounding Heaven and Earth.

Engine against th'Almighty. Sinner's tower.
Reversed thunder, Christ-side piercing-spear,
The six days' world transposing in an hour,
A kind of tune, which all things hear and fear,

Softness, and peace, and joy, and love, and bliss,
Exalted Manna, gladness of the best,
Heaven in ordinary, man well drest,
The Milky Way, the bird of Paradise,

Church-bells beyond the stars heard, the soul's blood,
The land of spices, something understood.

How about this for a summer romance poem? It is by Thomas Hood, once highly regarded for protest pieces like 'The Song of the Shirt' and copious light verse. But protest pieces rarely last and light verse is out of fashion, perhaps because there are no set societal norms to make fun of. The version of this lovely lyric in the old *Oxford Book of English Verse* – which admittedly probably kept it alive – is, incidentally, incomplete. Sir Arthur Quiller-Couch censored the last two stanzas. By 'peer' in the second last verse Hood simply means 'rival' or 'be equal to' – the poet's cheek is glowing like the roses in the twilight.

Time of Roses

by Thomas Hood

It was not in the winter
Our loving lot was cast;
It was the time of roses,
We plucked them as we passed.

That churlish season never frowned
On early lovers yet;
Oh no – the world was newly crowned
With flowers when first we met.

'Twas twilight, and I bade you go,
But still you held me fast.
It was the time of roses,
We plucked them as we passed.

What else could peer my glowing cheek
That tears began to stud?
And when I asked the like of love
You snatched a damask bud

And oped it to the dainty core
Still glowing to the last –
It was the time of roses,
We plucked them as we passed.

Housman published only two books of verse, *A Shropshire Lad*, in 1896, and *Last Poems*, twenty-six years later, in 1922. Though he was to live for another fourteen years, he apparently wrote no more poetry; and when his brother published a small collection after his death he had to call it *More Poems*.

This strange poem was originally included in *A Shropshire Lad*, but he deleted it in proof and it had to wait until *Last Poems* for its appearance in book form. It is susceptible to many interpretations, but Housman has provided us with a clue in a letter to a friend. 'The queen of air and darkness comes from a line of Coventry Patmore's "the powers of darkness and the air" which in its turn is a reference to "the prince of the power of the air" in the epistle to the Ephesians; and the meaning is Evil.'

'Her Strong Enchantments Failing ...'

by A. E. Housman

Her strong enchantments failing,
Her towers of fear in wreck,
Her limbecks dried of poisons
And the knife at her neck,

The Queen of air and darkness
Begins to shrill and cry,
'O young man, O my slayer,
To-morrow you shall die.'

O Queen of air and darkness,
I think 'tis truth you say,
And I shall die to-morrow;
But you will die to-day.

Valentin Iremonger belonged to the second wave of Irish modernism, the generation born about ten years after Beckett, Coffey and Devlin. Indeed he seemed for a while to be himself the second wave of Irish modernism, since there were few other modernists around; but, like most of those few, he too fell silent.

Daedalus in the Greek legend invented a method of flying by attaching waxed feathers to the arms, but poor old Icarus flew too near the sun, which naturally melted the wax, and he drowned. In the poem this may be the 'wrong story'. Icarus crashes because Daedalus was out in his calculations or botched the job. The adaptation of Greek legend to twentieth century realities was a favoured modernist device; and Joyce too used elements of the Daedalus myth.

Icarus

by Valentin Iremonger

As, even to-day, the airman, feeling the plane sweat
Suddenly, seeing the horizon tilt up gravely,
    the wings shiver
Knows that, for once, Daedalus has slipped up badly,
Drunk on the job perhaps, more likely dreaming,
    high flyer Icarus,
Head butting down, skidding along the light-shafts
Back, over the tones of the sea-waves and the slipstream,
    heard
The gravel-voiced, stuttering trumpets of his heart

Sennet among the crumbling courtyards of his brain
    the mistake
Of trusting somebody else on an important affair like this;
And while the flat sea, approaching, buckled into
    oh! avenues
Of acclamation, he saw the wrong story fan out into
    history,
Truth, undefined, lost in his own neglect. On the hills,
The summer-shackled hills, the sun spanged all day;
Love and the world were young and there was no ending.

But star-chaser, big-time-going, chancer Icarus
Like a dog on the sea lay and the girls forgot him,
And Daedalus, too busy hammering another job,
Remembered him only in pubs. No bugler at all
Sobbed taps for the young fool then, reported missing,
Presumed drowned, wing-bones and feathers on the tide,
Drifting in casually, one by one.

Patrick Kavanagh was thirty years dead when this appeared in the *Sunday Independent*. *Inniskeen Road: July Evening* comes from his first collection, *Ploughman and Other Poems*, published in Macmillan's Shilling Poets series in 1938. It is a direct expression of a common youthful experience of loneliness and isolation; and, though it is very expert, it is a young man's poem. No doubt he possessed the gift of laughter at the time, but he was unable to transmute it into his work. One has only to compare it with the way such experience is dealt with in *Tarry Flynn* to see the distance he still had to travel in this regard. Alexander Selkirk was a famous castaway, supposedly the model for Defoe's Robisnon Crusoe.

Inniskeen Road: July Evening

by Patrick Kavanagh

The bicycles go by in twos and threes —
There's a dance in Billy Brennan's barn tonight,
And there's the half-talk code of mysteries
And the wink-and-elbow language of delight.
Half-past eight and there is not a spot
Upon a mile of road, no shadow thrown
That might turn out a man or woman, not
A footfall tapping secrecies of stone.
I have what every poet hates in spite
Of all the solemn talk of contemplation.
Oh, Alexander Selkirk knew the plight
Of being king and government and nation.
A road, a mile of kingdom. I am king
Of banks and stones and every blooming thing.

This poem was first published in 1939, when Patrick Kavanagh was in his mid-thirties. In brief compass and almost solely through images, it manages to express loss, remorse and love; as well as a deep compassion for all other old men whom he sees as having been broken by life.

Memory Of My Father

by Patrick Kavanagh

Every old man I see
Reminds me of my father
When he had fallen in love with death
One time when sheaves were gathered.

That man I saw in Gardiner Street
Stumble on the kerb was one,
He stared at me half-eyed,
I might have been his son.

And I remember the musician
Faltering over his fiddle
In Bayswater, London,
He too set me the riddle.

Every old man I see
In October-coloured weather
Seems to say to me:
'I was once your father.'

Katherine Tynan was born four years before Yeats and was an early friend and confidante of his. Like him, she was prominently associated with what was called the Irish Literary Revival; and for some time her fame rivalled his own. Partly because she was married to the impecunious barrister, H. A. Hinkson, and was the principal bread-winner, she wrote an extraordinary number of novels, with title such as *What a Plague is Love* and *They Loved Greatly*. When he at length got a job as Resident Magistrate in County Mayo, they lived in a charming house, Brookhill, where John and Patricia Noone now live, outside Claremorris.

Slow Spring

By Katherine Tynan

O year, grow slowly. Exquisite, holy,
The days go on.
With almonds showing the pink stars blowing
And birds in the dawn.

Grow slowly year, like a child that is dear,
Or a lamb that is mild,
By little steps, and by little skips,
Like a lamb or a child.

T. E. Hulme published only six poems in his own lifetime. They appeared in 1912 in the pages of A. R. Orage's famous weekly, *The New Age*, as 'The Complete Poetical Works of T. E. Hulme'; but to the same journal he contributed many essays and observations which defined the modernism then still to come. The new poetry, he said, would be 'cheerful, dry and sophisticated'. Painting would become precise and geometric. In other works he was against the latter-day romanticism and impressionism which still dominated both arts. He was killed in action in 1917; but his insistence that modernism would be classical rather than romantic and his opposition to what he saw as the sloppinesses and sentimentalities of a democratic age had a profound influence on T. S. Eliot and Ezra Pound, who published the few additional poems which were found in his notebooks after his death.

Conversion

by T. E. Hulme

Light-hearted I walked into the valley wood
In the time of hyacinths,
Till beauty like a scented cloth
Cast over me, stifled me. I was bound
Motionless and faint of breath
By loveliness that is her own eunuch.

Now pass I to the final river
Ignominiously, in a sack, without sound,
As any peeping Turk to the Bosphorous.

This is a poem about the attempt to communicate experience, by a poet who severely limited his own efforts to do so. His poems were few and very compressed and, though he lived to be almost eighty, for the last forty years or so of his life William Empson added no more to the number he had already written. In fact this was one of the last.

He was in any case perhaps better known as a critic than a poet and his *Seven Types of Ambiguity* was one of the key texts of what was once known as 'the New Criticism'. After spending several years as a Professor of English in China and Japan, Empson returned to England to find that a school of poets known as 'the Movement' – which included Philip Larkin, Kingsley Amis, John Wain and many others – had adopted him as a sort of father figure. His comments on this phenomenon were not appreciated, any more than were his later attacks on the New Criticism for its neglect of biography as an aid to interpretation of a writer's work.

Let It Go

by William Empson

It is this deep blankness is the real thing strange.
The more things happen to you the more you can't
Tell or remember what they were.

The contradictions cover such a range.
The talk would talk and go so far aslant.
You don't want madhouse and the whole thing there.

Leigh Hunt has had a poor enough time of it from posterity, and since he didn't have much luck during his lifetime, it seems doubly unfair. Dickens caricatured him as the feckless Skimpole in *Bleak House*; Byron biographers have had fun with his arrival in Italy, in response to his lordship's invitations, accompanied by a large family on whose presence his lordship had not reckoned. But, in his lifetime, Hunt's troubles were largely the result of his clashes with tyrannical government authority over his activities as editor and publisher. He fought the good fight for liberty, tolerance and democracy in the reactionary England of his time more steadily than seemingly more dependable men; and he continued to write poetry when – because he had no money and that large family to support – he had no business to.

Jenny Kissed Me

by Leigh Hunt

Jenny kissed me when we met,
Jumping from the chair she sat in;
Time, you thief, who love to get
Sweets into you list, put that in!
Say I'm weary, say I'm sad,
Say that health and wealth have missed me,
Say I'm growing old, but add,
Jenny kissed me.

This was one of the most famous of Larkin's early poems. It was based on a paragraph in Edward Mayhew's great Victorian documentary classic, *London Labour and the London Poor*, which reads as follows:

'Of course I was drugged, and so heavily I did not regain my consciousness until the next morning. I was horrified to discover that I had been ruined, and for some days I was inconsolable, and cried like a child to be killed or sent back to my aunt.'

Originally called *The Less Deceived*, the poem provided the title for the book which first brought Larkin wide critical attention.

Deceptions

by Philip Larkin

Even so distant, I can taste the grief,
Bitter and sharp with stalks, he made you gulp.
The sun's occasional print, the brisk brief
Worry of wheels along the street outside
Where bridal London bows the other way,
And light, unanswerable and tall and wide,
Forbids the scar to heal, and drives
Shame out of hiding. All the unhurried day
Your mind lay open like a drawer of knives.

Slums, years have buried you. I would not dare
Console you if I could. What can be said,
Except that suffering is exact, but where
Desire takes charge, readings will grow erratic?
For you would hardly care
That you were less deceived, out on that bed,
Than he was, stumbling up the breathless stair
To burst into fulfilment's desolate attic.

For almost two centuries, poets have been expected to know about nature, to be able to recognise species of birds and trees at a glance, to be super-observant about the minutiae of leaves and petals. This expectation is vaguely supposed to derive from the work of the romantics, but a glance at Wordsworth will show that he is surprisingly undescriptive. In his poems, birds, trees and flowers are not as much described as evoked, often in very unparticular terms. The expectation really set in with the Victorian successors of the great 'nature poets'. Tennyson was a bit of a naturalist and so were many of the minor poets of the era. Their influence on critics was so great that Dylan Thomas felt he had to consult the encyclopaedia and stick in some descriptive details. David Wright's poem for Dannie Abse re-opens an old debate between poets about the degree of interest in nature which may be thought desirable for those who practise the art.

As You Were Saying

To Dannie Abse

By David Wright

I agree, Dannie, it's not important to know
The cognomens and purposes of greenery
Or birds (it's always a chaffinch or a sparrow;
Seagulls, I suppose, like blackbirds, are too easy).
The painter Rothenstein took Yeats for a walk
And found the visible world did not inspire
The poet, who apparently failed to remark
The abundant natural beauty of Gloucestershire,
But fixed his eyes in his boots and talked about
His concerns, which were not the noise of birds and water,
Or the sun, or the wildflowers, or the wind on the
    heath ...
The etceteras of nature preen and bloom – but the myopic
Celebrant of phenomena does not see them.

I live in the country now, having left London,
And find myself, very much to my surprise,
Reconnoitring the surrounding vegetation,
The local wildlife and even the night skies;
But not for the sake of poetry, thank goodness.
These things have forced themselves on me, being there.
One may as well find out about them. Who knows,
A night may come when I'll have need of the pole star.

Edwin Morgan has said that 'the two great opposing, unresolved, often interlocking themes of Stevenson's poetry are the desire for travel and the desire for home'. Nowhere is the desire for home – which was, of course, Scotland – better exemplified than in the well-known poem 'To S. R. Crockett'. The poem was written in the South Sea island of Vailima, where Stevenson ended his days, several months voyage away from his northern birthplace. Morgan has also said that the longing in it is 'not only longing for a place, but for a place with its history, even for a place in history'.

To S. R. Crockett

by Robert Louis Stevenson

Blows the wind today, and the sun and the rain are flying,
Blows the wind on the moors today and now,
Where about the graves of the martyrs the whaups
     are crying,
My heart remembers how!

Bare recumbent tombs of the dead in desert places,
Standing stones on the vacant wine-red moor,
Hills of sheep, and the howes of the silent vanished races,
And winds, austere and pure.

Be it granted to me to behold you again in dying,
Hills of home! And to hear again the call;
Hear about the graves of the martyrs the peewees crying,
And hear no more at all.

Francis Ledwidge was serving with the British army in France in 1916 when he wrote this beautiful elegy for Thomas MacDonagh, a fellow-poet who had been executed by a British army firing squad in Dublin on May 3rd of that year. Ledwidge himself was killed in action a little over a year later.

Such are, or were, the tragic ironies of Irish history. But perhaps the tentative prophecy of the last stanza is even now in some sense in the process of coming true.

As a poet too, Ledwidge was a product of the sort of divided culture which we are now learning to see as a source of enrichment rather than otherwise. Many of his poems are very English-pastoral, not to say English-Georgian. But the metaphor for Ireland here ('the dark cow') comes from a Gaelic tradition; as do the internal rhymes and assonances which give the poem much of its power.

Lament for Thomas MacDonagh

by Francis Ledwidge

He shall not hear the bittern cry
In the wild sky, where he is lain,
Nor voices of the sweeter birds
Above the wailing of the rain.

Nor shall he know when loud March blows
Thro' slanting snows her fanfare shrill,
Blowing to flame the golden cup
Of many an upset daffodil.

But when the Dark Cow leaves the moor,
And pastures poor with greedy weeds,
Perhaps he'll hear her low at morn
Lifting her horn in pleasant meads.

Ledwidge's early poems were published in the *Drogheda Independent*, just as Patrick Kavanagh's were in the *Dundalk Democrat*; but the difference between this and, say, 'Inniskeen Road: July Evening' is more than the difference between two temperaments: it is the difference between two literatures, one of which has declared its independence. Lovely and seemingly uncontrived though this is, it is an English Georgian poem, even to the gipsy and the farmer's boy. It was in fact published in Edward Marsh's famous *Georgian Anthology* in 1916, the year before the poet's death in what Lloyd George called 'the war to end all wars'.

June

by Francis Ledwidge

Broom out the floor now, lay the fender by,
And plant this bee-sucked bough of woodbine there,
And let the window down. The butterfly
Floats in upon the sunbeam, and the fair
Tanned face of June, the nomad gipsy, laughs
Above her widespread wares, the while she tells
The farmers' fortune in the fields and quaffs
The water from the spider-peopled wells.

The hedges are all drowned in green grass seas,
And bobbing poppies flare like Elmo's light,
While siren-like the pollen-stained bees
Drone in the clover depths. And up the height
The cuckoo's voice is hoarse and broke with joy,
And on the lowland crops the crows made raid,
Nor fear the clappers of the farmer's boy,
Who sleeps, like drunken Noah, in the shade.

And loop this red rose in that hazel ring
That snares your little ear, for June is short
And we must joy in it and dance and sing.
And from her bounty draw her rosy worth.
Ay! Soon the swallows will be flying south,
The wind wheel north to gather in the snow,
Even the roses split on youth's red mouth
Will soon blow down the road all roses go.

'Our Lady of Walsingham' used to be part of Lowell's famous elegy for his cousin Warren Winslow, where it provided a calm and comparatively lucid interval amid the tumultuous and somewhat obscure agonisings of the longer work. Then he decided it should stand as a separate poem.

Walsingham is a Norfolk village where the Virgin Mary was said to have appeared in the Middle Ages. It became a place of pilgrimage for worshippers from all over Europe and continued to be so even after the Reformation.

Lowell, who was a Catholic at the time, does not seem to have visited Walsingham, but Warren Winslow, who was in the navy, apparently did. Lowell was struck by a passage in E. I. Watkin's *Catholic Art and Culture* and even took the description of the 'expressionless' statue of the Virgin from Watkin. In other words, in part at least, he versified a passage from someone else's prose – a commoner practise among authors of long poems than one might suppose. But whatever he did, the result is evocative, tender and haunting.

Our Lady of Walsingham

by Robert Lowell

There once the penitents took off their shoes
And then walked barefoot the remaining mile;
And the small trees, a stream and hedgerows file
Slowly along the munching English lane,
Like cows to the old shrine, until you lose
Track of your dragging pain.
The stream flows down under the druid tree,
Shiloah's whirlpools gurgle and make glad
The castle of God. Sailor, you were glad
And whistled Sion by that stream. But see:

Our Lady, too small for her canopy,
Sits near the altar. There's no comeliness
At all or charm in that expressionless
Face with its heavy eyelids. As before,
This face, for centuries a memory,
Non est species, neque decor,
Expressionless, expresses God: it goes
Past castled Sion. She knows what God knows,
Not Calvary's Cross nor crib at Bethlehem
Now, and the world shall come to Walsingham.

Alice Meynell does not get much of a look-in these days, even among feminist critics who are laudably anxious to reinstate the neglected. Perhaps this is because she is a religious poet; perhaps because her life was quiet and respectable and she was, in her way, successful.

She and her husband Wilfred were central figures in Edwardian literary and Catholic London. They discovered Francis Thompson, a drug addict and drunkard who was sleeping rough on the Embankment, rehabilitated and published him; and perhaps some of the neglect of Alice's own poetry is also traceable to the fact that she proclaimed Thompson a great genius. It is always dangerous to serve other people's reputations.

Although she was a Catholic, Alice Meyell's essentially religious poetry speaks to people who do not share her religious views. I think this is because, Catholic or otherwise, it respects the mystery of existence, as this marvellous poem does. Indeed one could see it as existentialist.

'I Am The Way'

by Alice Meynell

Thou are the Way.
Hadst thou been nothing but the goal
I cannot say
If Thou hadst ever ever met my soul.

I cannot see —
I, child of process – if there lies
An end for me,
Full of repose, full of replies.

I'll not reproach
The road that winds, my feet that err.
Access, Approach
Art Thou, Time, Way, and Wayfarer.

'Thalassa' was Louis MacNeice's last poem, found among his papers after his death in 1963. Thalassa is the Greek word for the sea.

Life as a voyage of peril and discovery on which we must all set out — and which we must resume again even after shipwreck — is an idea which many other poets have adopted since Homer described such a voyage in the *Odyssey*.

But poems such as Tennyson's marvellous 'Ulysses' had been more informed by idealism and self-regard than MacNeice's version is. His mariners are called on to fare forth again in spite of disillusion, failure and an uncomfortable degree of self-knowledge.

At the time he wrote it, MacNeice was not in good shape. He was drinking too much and in many ways fed up. But in spite of everything he had a sort of incurable optimism about the world. And he was a man of courage. I think it is a noble last poem for such a bruised and disillusioned voyager to have written.

Thalassa

by Louis MacNeice

Run out the boat, my broken comrades;
Let the old seaweed crack, the surge
Burgeon oblivious of the last
Embarkation of feckless men,
Let every adverse force converge —
Here we must needs embark again.

Run up the sail, my heartsick comrades;
Let each horizon tilt and lurch —
You know the worst; your wills are fickle,
Your values blurred, your hearts impure
And your past life a ruined church —
But let your poison be your cure.

Put out to sea, ignoble comrades,
Whose record shall be noble yet;
Butting through scarps of moving marble
The narwhal dares us to be free;
By a high star our course is set,
Our end is Life. Put out to sea.

The English Victorians liked pairs. Hence they had Gladstone and Disraeli; Dickens and Thackeray; Tennyson and Browning; Hardy and Meredith. Meredith was inclined to regret that his fame as a novelist had outstripped his reputation as a poet. Now all his laurels have faded, but it must be said that some of his poetry seems to have survived better than his prose. *Love in the Valley* was included in his first book, *Poems*, published in 1851.

from Love in the Valley

by George Meredith

Lovely are the curves of the white owl sweeping
Wavy in the dusk lit by one large star,
Lone on the fir-branch, his rattle-note unvaried,
Brooding o'er the gloom, spins the brown eve-jar.
Darker grows the valley, more and more forgetting:
So were it with me, if forgetting could be willed.
Tell the grassy hollow that holds the bubbling well-spring,
Tell it to forget the source that keeps it filled.

Stepping down the hill with her fair companions,
Arm in arm, all against the raying West,
Boldly she sings, to the merry tune she marches,
Brave in her shape, and sweeter unpossessed.
Sweeter, for she is what my heart first awaking
Whispered the world was; morning light is she.
Love that so desires would fain keep her changeless;
Fain would fling the net, and fain have her free.

*

Could I find a place to be alone with heaven,
I would speak my heart out: heaven is my need.
Every woodland tree is flushing like the dogwood,
Flashing like the whitebeam, swaying like the reed.
Flushing like the dogwood crimson in October;
Streaming like the flag-reed South-West blown;
Flashing as in gusts the sudden lighted white-beam:
All seem to know what is for heaven alone.

The title should not be taken too seriously. Blake believed that the Christian orthodoxy as propagated was a vast system of suppression of man's natural instincts, which he thought were good. To call attention to this he sometimes reversed the terminology. The 'Proverbs of Hell' are from a longer work, 'The Marriage of Heaven and Hell'. It could be objected that they are not poetry; and some of them are not even good advice; but they are all, in some sense, illuminating and refreshing; and perhaps they are all good advice for the Poetic Genius which Blake also believed to be present in every human being. This is the first section of the proverbs.

Proverbs of Hell

by William Blake

In seed time learn, in harvest teach, in winter enjoy.
Drive your cart and your plow over the bones of the dead.
The road of excess leads to the palace of wisdom.
Prudence is a rich ugly old maid courted by Incapacity.
He who desires but acts not, breeds pestilence.
The cut worm forgives the plow.
Dip him in the river who loves water.
A fool sees not the same tree as a wise man sees.
He whose face gives no light, shall never become a star.
Eternity is in love with the productions of time.
The busy bee has no time for sorrow.
The hours of folly are measured by the clock; but of
      wisdom, no clock can measure.
All wholesome food is caught without a net or a trap.
Bring out number, weight and measure in a year of dearth.
No bird soars too high, if he soars with his own wings.
A dead body revenges not injuries.
The most sublime act is to set another before you.
If the fool would persist in his folly he would become wise.
Folly is the cloak of knavery.
Shame is Pride's cloak.

Coventry Patmore was the Victorian laureate of wedded bliss. He wrote a long poem about his first marriage, whose title, *The Angel In The House*, just about sums it up. His first wife bore him six children; his second brought him both money and religious certainty, for she was wealthy as well as devout and under her influence he converted to Catholicism. After her death he married his children's governess.

As he grew older his meditations on marital matters became more mystical and, in an obscure way, more erotic; but he destroyed some of them on the advice of his confessor, whose name was Gerard Manley Hopkins.

Those who have a taste for that most neglected of poetic forms, the novel in verse, might find parts of *The Angel In The House* still readable, but some of Patmore's shorter pieces, of which this is an example, are superb.

Magna Est Veritas

by Coventry Patmore

Here, in this little Bay,
Full of tumultuous life and great repose,
Where, twice a day,
The purposeless glad ocean comes and goes,
Under high cliffs, and far from the huge town,
I sit me down.
For want of me the world's course will not fail;
When all its work is done, the lie shall rot;
The truth is great, and shall prevail,
When none cares whether is prevail or not.

To say that Laura Riding has had a bad press in recent decades would be an understatement. She believed in the 'patriarchal leer', the patronising and sometimes openly hostile way in which men regarded women of achievement. Whether or not there is such a thing, the gaze that has been turned on her has been for the most part virulently hostile. In book after book she has been portrayed as a voracious egotist who wrecked other people's lives, probably thought she was a god, was possibly a witch and was certainly insane.

Perhaps even worse from her point of view, her own work has been often derided or ignored. To many critics, she is simply part of Robert Graves's story, the peculiar object of his infatuation, who for reasons they find hard to explain was his errant, ungovernable muse and the inspiration of his theories about the White Goddess.

A part of literary history therefore, but not through her own work and always with the implication that it was of secondary importance.

Fortunately, though, the poetry is still there: cool, truth-seeking, sane; and often, beneath its elliptical opacities, immensely wise.

The Wind Suffers

by Laura Riding

The wind suffers of blowing,
The sea suffers of water,
And fire suffers of burning,
And I of a living name.

As stone suffers of stoniness,
As light of its shiningness,
As birds of their wingedness,
So I of my whoness.

And what is the cure of all this?
What the not and not suffering?
What the better and later of this?
What the more me of me?

How for the pain-world to be
More world and no pain?
How for the old rain to fall
More wet and more dry?

How for the wilful blood to run
More salt-red and sweet-white?
And for me in my actualness
To more shriek and more smile?

By no other miracles,
By the same knowing poison,
By an improved anguish,
By my further dying.

Robert Louis Stevenson was the finest prose writer of the late nineteenth century and, though he wrote comparatively few poems, his better ones are worthy of his genius. He decided early to live by other tenets than those of the strict Scottish Calvinism in which he was brought up, but remained concerned with questions relating to it, including, of course, justification by faith. Here he spells out the faith which, in spite of his clear-sighted knowledge of things, he still holds; and asks the Lord if that will suffice. Underlying the poem is a sort of melancholy, ironic acknowledgement that the mentors of his youth would answer, 'No'. In spite of a tendency to rhetorical generalisation in the language and an over-free use of martial metaphor – both essentially Victorian failings – it is a very fine poem. Many poets have tried to make professions of faith of one kind or another. Few have succeeded half as well.

If This Were Faith

by Robert Louis Stevenson

God, if this were enough,
That I see things bare to the buff
And up to the buttocks in mire,
That I ask nor hope nor hire,
Nut in the husk,
Nor dawn beyond death;
God, if this were faith!

Having felt thy wind in my face
Spit sorrow and disgrace,
Having seen thine evil doom
In Golgotha and Khartoum,
And the brutes, the work of thine hands,
Fill with injustice lands
And stain with blood the sea:
If still in my veins the glee
Of the black night and the sun
And the lost battle, run:
If, an adept,
The iniquitous lists I still accept
With joy, and joy to endure and be withstood,
And still do battle and perish for a dream of good:
God, if that were enough?

If to feel, in the ink of the slough,
And the sink of the mire,
Veins of glory and fire
Run through and transpierce and transpire,

And a secret purpose of glory in every part,
And the answering glory of battle fill my heart;
To thrill with the joy of girded men,
To go on for ever and fail and go on again,
And be mauled to the earth and arise,
And contend for the shade of a word and a thing
    not seen with the eyes:
With the half of a broken hope for a pillow at night
That somehow the right is the right
And the smooth shall bloom from the rough:
Lord, if that were enough?

Critics have debated whether Yeats was the greater poet of friendship or of love. He thought himself that he was a poet of hate, declaring that hatred was his principal inspiration and describing how he sat at his desk, 'rocking' himself 'into hatred' as part of the inspirational process. There is certainly a good deal of hate in *The Fisherman*, which is, I am glad to learn, or was until recently, still in the schoolbooks, in spite of the fact that to hate anything or anybody, except two or three approved objects, is nowadays to incur serious disapproval.

Yeats's targets are still there, though there is a sort of general denial that 'great art' is any longer 'beaten down', and plenty of government agencies to assure us that it isn't so.

The alternative audience is a dream of every poet worth his or her salt. We may find Yeats's alternative – peasant or country gentleman? – a little unsatisfactory; but the point about him is that he is not a professional poetry-lover. To every poet his or her own imagined alternative.

The Fisherman

by W. B. Yeats

Although I can see him still,
The freckled man who goes
To a grey place on a hill
In grey Connemara clothes
At dawn to catch his flies,
It's long since I began
To call up to the eyes
This wise and simple man.
All day I'd looked in the face
What I had hoped 'twould be
To write for my own race
And the reality;
The living men that I hate,
The dead man that I loved,
The craven man in his seat,
The insolent unreproved,
And no knave brought to book
Who has won a drunken cheer,
The witty man and his joke
Aimed at the commonest ear,
The clever man who cries
The catch-cries of the clown,
The beating down of the wise
And great Art beaten down.

Maybe a twelvemonth since
Suddenly I bcgan,
In scorn of this audience,

Imagining a man,
And his sun-freckled face,
And grey Connemara cloth,
Climbing up to a place
Where stone is dark under froth,
And the down-turn of his wrist
When the flies drop in the stream;
A man who does not exist,
A man who is but a dream;
And cried, 'Before I am old
I shall have written him one
Poem maybe as cold
And passionate as the dawn.'

Though other poets may have achieved a sometimes peculiar degree of sanctity, Robert Southwell is the only English poet of distinction to have been actually canonised as a saint; and he only gained the distinction a few years ago in company with a large number of fellow Jesuits, all martyrs in the reign of Elizabeth the First of England. Most of his poems were written in the Tower of London, where he was imprisoned and repeatedly tortured for about three years before being beheaded at the age of thirty-four. This one is less devotional than some of the others; and has a sort of secular cheerfulness about it.

Times Go By Turns

by Robert Southwell

The lopped tree in time may grow again,
Most naked plants renew both fruit and flower;
The sorriest wight may find release of pain,
The driest soil suck in some moistening shower.
Times go by turns, and chances change by course,
From foul to fair, from better hap to worse.

The sea of fortune doth not ever flow,
She draws her favours to the lowest ebb,
Her tides hath equal times to come and go,
Her loom doth weave the fine and coarsest web.
No joy so great but runneth to an end,
No hap so hard but may in fine amend.

Not always fall of leaf, nor ever spring,
No endless night, yet not eternal day;
The saddest birds a season find to sing,
The roughest storm a calm may soon allay.
Thus, with succeeding turns, God tempereth all,
That man may hope to rise, yet fear to fall.

A chance may win that by mischance was lost;
The net that holds no great, takes little fish;
In some things all, in all things none are crossed;
Few all they need, but none have all they wish.
Unmeddled joys here to no man befall;
Who least, hath some; who most, hath never all.

Shelley is a bit of a problem. To many he is an apostle of human progress, born before his time but bravely propagating a gospel of liberty, equality, free love and the rights of women. Others point to his aristocratic disdain for the practicalities of existence and the fact that he treated his own women very badly. While many regard him as a genius, his poetry too has been criticised by some of the best poetic practitioners of our time for its cloudiness, imprecision and rhetoric.

In its compression and irony, 'Ozymandias' is by no means typical of his work. The sting is in the brilliant ambiguity of the last line. Are the 'mighty' who look upon Ozymandias's works to despair because they can never emulate them? Or because Ozymandias was mortal and this is all that is left of him and his power?

Ozymandias

by Percy Bysshe Shelley

I met a traveller from an antique land
Who said — Two vast and trunkless legs of stone
Stand in the desert ... Near them, on the sand,
Half sunk a shattered visage lies, whose frown,
And wrinkled lip, and sneer of cold command,
Tell that its sculptor well those passions read
Which yet survive, stamped on these lifeless things,
The hand that mocked them, and the heart that fed;
And on the pedestal, these words appear:
'My name is Ozymandias, king of kings:
Look on my works, ye Mighty, and despair!'
Nothing beside remains. Round the decay
Of that colossal wreck, boundless and bare
The lone and level sands stretch far away.

The last lines of Stevie Smith's *Not Waving But Drowning* are among the few lines of contemporary poetry that have entered the popular consciousness.

Stevie Smith lived for most of her life with an elderly aunt in a north London suburb, Palmer's Green, and worked for many years as secretary to the magazine publisher, George Newnes – 'It is the privilege of the rich to waste the time of the poor,' she wrote.

She had some success early on with a novel called *Novel On Yellow Paper*, but like many poets she suffered neglect in middle-age; and when *X*, a magazine with which I was associated, published her poems in the late Fifties and early Sixties she was in the doldrums. Partly as a result of *X*, towards the end she enjoyed a great flowering, reading – and singing – her poems in the Albert Hall and elsewhere.

Though we had some very jolly meetings and did a couple of memorable readings together, I did not know her well – who did? – but to know her at all was to love her. Like her poems she was eccentric, brave, sad, funny and beautiful.

She does not lack readers, but she has not yet been fully recognised in literary circles for what she is – one of the truly great originals of English poetry.

Not Waving But Drowning

by Stevie Smith

Nobody heard him, the dead man,
But still he lay moaning:
I was much further out than you thought
And not waving but drowning.

Poor chap, he always loved larking
And now he's dead
It must have been too cold for him, his heart gave way
They said.

Oh, no no no, it was too cold always
(Still the dead one lay moaning)
I was much too far out all my life
And not waving but drowning.

It had not been my intention to include poems by living poets in this anthology, but I made an exception in favour of Francis Stuart's beautiful poem about Ireland, partly because he was ninety-four and partly because that particular edition of the *Sunday Independent* was published on St Patrick's Day.

Francis returned to poetry after a long literary lifetime largely given over to novels; indeed, in that year, his ninety-fourth, he had published a new book of poems, *Arrow of Anguish*. His first book, *We Have Kept the Faith*, appeared in 1923; and there was then no other until a Selected Poems appeared nearly sixty years later, in 1982. The poet in him has been re-born in extreme old age and during the last two decades of his life he wrote a handful of short lyrics which would, even if he had written nothing else, assure him of literary immortality.

'Ireland', written in Berlin in 1943, is one of the few poems he wrote between youth and old age. In the twentieth century it has been very difficult to write poems in praise of anything, or expressing one's love of anything, let alone one's native land; but this poem evokes Ireland and expresses a love for it in an entirely natural and convincing way.

Ireland

by Francis Stuart

Over you falls the sea light, festive yet pale
As though from the trees hung candles alight in a gale
To fill with shadows your days, as the distant beat
Of waves fills the lonely width of many a western street.
Bare and grey and hung with berries of mountain ash,
Drifting through ages with tilted fields awash,
Steeped with your few lost lights in the long Atlantic dark,
Sea-birds' shelter, our shelter and ark.

One of the most remarkable things about Francis Stuart was that he became a poet again in the last two decades of his long life, and a much finer one than he had been in his youth. His first volume, *We Have Kept The Faith*, was published in 1923, when he was twenty-one, and won the Tailteann Prize, a government-sponsored prize for poetry, in that year. He would be at some pains to avoid this kind of success in the years to come; and no more poems appeared in volume form until Raven Arts re-published the original volume with a number of new poems for his eightieth birthday in 1982. It was followed by another edition containing additional poems ten years later. This sombre, penetrating poem, which expresses a deep and unpalatable truth about our time, was published in his ninetieth year.

The Great

by Francis Stuart

The great are not great now, the good are not good;
All who are named, who appear in the eye of day
Are touched by the rot, are lipped and lapped by the flood
Of our downfall. Black is the hidden ray
Of the good and great in our time. Unknown
Are their voices, their faces are turned, do not shine.
All that shines in this air is complacent, bone
Of the bright dry bone, and the blight of the brine
Of the desert is in them. Names in the mouths of men
Are wormy. The great are the others, are those
Gathered as though asleep, those beyond ken,
Growing by far, small streams as the willow grows.

Christopher Smart believed that everything in the world demonstrated the existence of a beneficent creator. He was, of course, mad, and was accordingly locked up several times in the awful madhouses of the eighteenth century. On one of these occasions he wrote fragments of a long poem called *Jubilate Agno*, from which these lines about his cat Jeoffry are taken. His best epitaph was supplied by Samuel Johnson, who reproved Boswell for speaking of Smart's madness: 'They told me Kit Smart was mad, sir, because he desired people to pray with him in the street and because he wore dirty shirts. As for the first, I would as lief pray with Kit Smart as with any man. And as for the second, I have no great passion for clean linen myself.'

from Jubilato Agno

by Christopher Smart

For I will consider my Cat Jeoffry,
For he is the servant of the Living God duly and daily
serving him.
For at the first glance of the glory of God in the East he
worships in his way.
For this is done by wreathing his body seven times round
with elegant quickness.
For first he looks upon his forepaws to see if they are clean.
For secondly he kicks up behind to clear away there.
For thirdly he works it upon stretch with the forepaws
extended.
For fourthly he sharpens his paws by wood.
For fifthly he washes himself.
For sixthly he rolls upon wash.
For seventhly he fleas himself, that he may not be
interrupted upon the beat.
For eightly he rubs himself against a post.
For ninthly he looks up for his instructions.
For tenthly he goes in quest of food.
For he counteracts the powers of darkness by his electrical
skin and glaring eyes.
For he counteracts the Devil, who is death, by brisking
about the life.
For he is of the tribe of Tiger.
For he purrs in thankfulness, when God tells him he is a
good cat.

I know little of Chidiock Tichborne except that he was beheaded in the Tower of London in 1586, in the reign of Queen Elizabeth, when he was aged about thirty. He is supposed to have written this sombrely magnificent poem the night before he died. Perhaps he did; no doubt the prospect of being beheaded would concentrate the mind wonderfully; but it seems to express truths – a view of life and perhaps particularly an unpopular, one could almost say Beckett-like, view of youth – which are not contingent on the immediate circumstance.

Elegy

by Chidiock Tichborne

My prime of youth is but a frost of cares.
My feast of joy is but a dish of pain,
My crop of corn is but a field of tares,
And all my good is but vain hope of gain.
The day is past and yet I saw no sun,
And now I live, and now my life is done.

My tale was heard and yet it was not told,
My fruit is fallen and yet my leaves are green;
My youth is spent and yet I am not old,
I saw the world and yet I was not seen.
My thread is cut and yet it is not spun,
And now I live, and now my life is done.

I sought my death and found it in my womb,
I looked for life and saw it was a shade;
I trod the earth and knew it was my tomb,
And now I die, and now I was but made.
My glass is full, and now my glass is run,
And now I live, and now my life is done.

This famous poem had its origin in a walking tour Wordsworth and his sister Dorothy took in the Scottish Highlands in 1803; but it is not at all certain that there ever was such a girl as the one described. It was harvest-time and there were men and women reapers working in the small Highland fields; but he had been reading a book called *A Tour in Scotland* by a certain Thomas Wilkinson, in which the author described seeing a girl reaping alone and singing by herself as she worked: 'She sang in Erse, as she bended over her sickle; the sweetest human voice I ever heard; her strains were tenderly melancholy, and felt delicious, long after they were heard no more.' As can be seen, Wordsworth took over this sentence and made a melodically haunting and beautiful poem out of it.

The Solitary Reaper

by William Wordsworth

Behold her, single in the field,
Yon solitary Highland Lass!
Reaping and singing by herself;
Stop here, or gently pass!
Alone she cuts and binds the grain,
And sings a melancholy strain;
O listen! For the vale profound
Is overflowing with the sound.

Will no-one tell me what she sings? —
Perhaps the plaintive numbers flow
For old, unhappy, far-off things,
And battles long ago:
Or is it some more humble lay,
Familiar matter of to-day?
Some natural sorrow, loss, or pain,
That has been and may be again?

Whate'er the theme the maiden sang
As if the song could have no ending;
I saw her singing at her work,
And o'er the sickle bending; —
I listened, motionless and still;
And, as I mounted up the hill,
The music in my heart I bore,
Long after it was heard no more.

Shakespeare's sonnets are a bit of a problem. Academic scholars have to admire them all, but the rest of us may think that some of them sound false and that a lot of the others are plain boring – after all, who cares whether the Earl of Southampton was going to perpetuate his line, through the begetting of a male heir with a suitable lady, or not?

But a handful are among the greatest short poems ever written. There is no mistaking the sincerity of this catalogue of human sorrows and regrets, or indeed of the loving grace-note with which it ends.

Sonnet

by William Shakespeare

When to the sessions of sweet silent thought
I summon up remembrance of things past,
I sigh the lack of many a thing I sought,
And with old woes new wail my dear time's waste:
Then can I drown an eye, unused to flow,
For precious friends hid in death's dateless night,
And weep afresh love's long-since-cancelled woe
And moan th' expense of many a vanished sight.
Then can I grieve at grievances foregone
And heavily from woe to woe tell o'er
The sad account of fore bemoanèd moan,
Which I new pay as if not paid before.

But if the while I think on thee, dear friend,
All losses are restored and sorrows end.

W. H. Auden said that, 'Probably more nonsense has been talked and written, more intellectual and emotional energy expended in vain, on the sonnets of Shakespeare than on any other literary work in the world.' What Auden was principally objecting to was the endless speculation about the identities of the 'dark lady' and 'Mr. W. H.', and their relationship to each other and to William Shakespeare.

Whoever they were, they had some astonishing and, it must be said, some very boring poems addressed to them. This is one of the more beautiful – wonderfully frank and true in its opening octet; equally true, or at least true-seeming, in its apparently heart-felt sextet. How consoling it is to know that Shakespeare was envious of other people's talents, that he desired 'this man's art and that man's scope', and undervalued the very gifts that we now find so dazzling. (Eliot appropriated these lines, as he appropriated so much else, presumably as a way of confessing that he too shared such envious feelings.) But how true also to the central fact of a lover's existence are the six lines of the sextet.

Sonnet

by William Shakespeare

When, in disgrace with Fortune and men's eyes,
I all alone beweep my outcast state,
And trouble deaf Heaven with my bootless cries,
And look upon myself and curse my fate,
Wishing me like to one more rich in hope,
Featured like him, like him with friends possessed,
Desiring this man's art, and that man's scope,
With what I most enjoy contented least;

Yet in these thoughts myself almost despising,
Haply I think on thee, and then my state,
Like to the lark at break of day arising
From sullen earth, sings hymns at Heaven's gate;
For thy sweet love remembered such wealth brings,
That then I scorn to change my state with kings.

Ford Madox Ford, who knew the Rossetti family as a child, has left us a picture of Christina, writing her poems 'on the corner of the cracked washstand in the fireless top back bedroom', while her brothers entertained their literary friends downstairs, adding for good measure that the poems were written 'on the backs of old letters'.

The description is perhaps rather fanciful. Christina's brother, Dante Gabriel Rossetti, was indeed the centre of an admiring circle of other poets and painters before the fates that attend the most brilliant began their work and brandy and chloral became his refuge and his doom.

But she herself was by no means unknown in Pre-Raphaelite circles. She published her first book before Dante did, and two other books appeared in her lifetime.

She was nothing but a poet. After an unsuccessful foray as a governess she never sought other employment again. And after turning down an offer of marriage from the Pre-Raphaelite painter James Collinson she entertained no other suitors, though a recent biographer has suggested a hopeless love for another Pre-Raphaelite, William Bell Scott, who was married when she met him.

She was a devout High Anglican; and, as C. H. Sisson has put it, rather 'churchy' as well as religious; but 'Up-Hill' — stoic, grim, but strangely encouraging, even humourous — could have been written by an unbeliever. What is really remarkable about it is the conversational rhythm. It is the rhythm which makes it one of the most memorable — in the sense of haunting — poems ever written. Read it once and you're hooked.

Up-Hill

by Christina Rossetti

Does the road wind up-hill all the way?
  Yes, to the very end.
Will the day's journey take the whole long day?
  From morn to night, my friend.

But is there for the night a resting-place?
  A roof for when the slow dark hours begin.
May not the darkness hide it from my face?
  You cannot miss that inn.

Shall I meet no other wayfarers at night?
  Those who have gone before.
Then must I knock, or call when just in sight?
  They will not keep you standing at that door.

Shall I find comfort, travel-sore and weak?
  Of labour you shall find the sum.
Will there be beds for me and all who seek?
  Yea, beds for all who come.

William Wordsworth disappointed his few remaining radical–liberal admirers by accepting a Civil List pension in 1842 and the laureateship six months later. Among these radicals was the young Robert Browning, who saw himself as the heir to the great generation just passed, that of Byron, Shelley, Hazlitt and Leigh Hunt – and who, unlike poor Wordsworth, had independent means. In later life he more or less admitted that Wordsworth's supposed apostasy was the occasion of his poem, but spoke of having 'in his hasty youth' adopted 'a very great and famous man' as a 'sort of painter's model'.

The Lost Leader

by Robert Browning

Just for a handful of silver he left us,
Just for a riband to stick in his coat —
Found the one gift of which fortune bereft us,
Lost all the others she lets us devote;
They, with the gold to give, doled him out silver,
So much was theirs who so little allowed;
How all our copper had gone for his service!
Rags — were they purple, his heart had been proud!
We that had loved him so, followed him, honoured him,
Lived in his mind and magnificent eye,
Learned his great language, caught his clear accents,
Made him our pattern to live and to die!
Shakespeare was of us, Milton was for us,
Burns, Shelley were with us — they watch from their
    graves!
He alone breaks from the van and the freemen,
— He alone sinks to the rear and the slaves!

We shall march prospering — not through his presence;
Songs may inspirit us — not from his lyre;
Deeds will be done — while he boasts his quiescence,
Still bidding crouch whom the rest bade aspire;
Blot out his name, then, record one lost soul more,
One more devils' triumph and sorrow for angels,
One wrong more to man, one more insult to God!
Life's night begins; let him never come back to us!
There would be doubt, hesitation, and pain,
Forced praise on our part — the glimmer of twilight,

Never glad confident morning again!
Best fight on well, for we taught him – strike gallantly,
Menace our heart ere we master his own;
Then let him receive the new knowledge and wait us,
Pardoned in heaven, the first by the throne!

Brought up in a remote Lincolnshire rectory presided over by an alcoholic and sometimes violent father, all three Tennyson brothers became poets. As boys, Alfred and Charles roamed the Lincolnshire fields shouting couplets at each other across the hedgerows.

Neither Frederick nor Charles achieved the same eminence as Alfred. (No poet had ever achieved the same eminence as Alfred; and, it is pretty safe to say no poet ever will again, for we do not accord the same reverence to our great in any sphere as the Victorians did.) But Charles at least is now, to some small degree, in fashion; and, in so far as the poem makes a prophesy, it has, to some small degree, come true.

Charles changed his name to Tennyson Turner to accommodate the wishes of a relative who left him money. He was an opium addict and suffered several disappointments in life before enjoying a relatively peaceful last period as an eccentric country clergyman – like his father, but less resentful of the world. When he died in 1879 he left behind some 342 sonnets, which were published with this lovely poem by Alfred as a preface. The occasion was in itself a worthy one, but the poem, I think, far transcends it.

Prefatory Poem To My Brother's Sonnets

by Alfred Tennyson

Midnight, June 30, 1879

1.

Midnight — in no midsummer tune
The breakers lash the shores:
The cuckoo of a joyless June
Is calling out of doors:

And thou hast vanished from thine own
To that which looks like rest,
True brother, only to be known
By those who love thee best.

2.

Midnight — and joyless June gone by,
And from the deluged park
The cuckoo of a worse July
Is calling through the dark:

But thou art silent underground,
And o'er thee streams the rain,
True poet, surely to be found
When Truth is found again.

3.

And now to these unsummered skies
The summer bird is still,
Far off a phantom cuckoo cries
From out a phantom hill;

And through this midnight breaks the sun
Of sixty years away,
The light of days when life begun,
The days that scem today,

When all my griefs were shared with thee,
As all my hopes were thine —
As all thou wert were one with me,
May all thou art be mine!

It seems incredible that Tennyson wrote *Ulysses* during his twenty-fourth year. In it he imagines the Homeric wanderer safe at home in Ithaca, 'an idle king,' who 'matched with an aged wife,' must 'mete and dole/Unequal laws unto a savage race/That hoard and sleep and feed and know not me.' He has been on equal terms with the heroes, seen many cities and has 'become a name,' who can claim to be himself 'not least, but honoured of them all.'

And so he leaves the government of the little island to his son Telemachus, summons his old comrades and asks them to set forth again in search of whatever voyaging may bring. This deliberately exploratory and questing aspect of the Ulyssean character is not in the *Odyssey*, where the struggle is to get back home and stay there. As Tennyson presents it, it is even somewhat nineteenth-century in tone, relating to the sort of scientific and philosophical enquiry which was so much a part of his own era. But his great poem is nevertheless quite convincing and amply deserves its place in innumerable anthologies.

from Ulysses

by Alfred Tennyson

There lies the port; the vessel puffs her sail:
There gloom and dark broad seas. My mariners,
Souls that have toiled, and wrought, and thought
    with me —
That ever with a frolic welcome took
The thunder and the sunshine, and opposed
Free hearts, free foreheads — you and I are old;
Old age hath yet his honour and his toil;
Death closes all: but something ere the end,
Some work of noble note, may yet be done,
Not unbecoming men that strove with Gods.
The lights begin to twinkle from the rocks:
The long day wanes: the slow moon climbs: the deep
Moans round with many voices. Come, my friends,
'Tis not too late to seek a newer world.
Push off, and sitting well in order smite
The sounding furrows; for my purpose holds
To sail beyond the sunset, and the baths
Of all the western stars, until I die.
It may be that the gulfs will wash us down:
It may be we shall touch the Happy Isles,
And see the great Achilles, whom we knew.
Though much is taken, much abides, and though
We are not now that strength which in old days
Moved earth and heaven; that which we are, we are;
One equal temper of heroic hearts,
Made weak by time and fate, but strong in will
To strive, to seek, to find, and not to yield.

Christmas is responsible for torrents of bad verse, amply, if not intentionally, expressing the sentimentality and duplicity of heart with which the Christmas story and the whole Christian myth are now regarded in our society. Some poets, most notably Thomas Hardy, have written sincerely out of what might be called a nostalgia for faith and the simplicities of belief. Paul Durcan has published a remarkable poem about the loneliness which is the primary emotion that Christmas brings to many people.

But there are very few unfussy and unreserved acceptances of the Christmas story in contemporary poetry; and few which express the truths of the myth, even on a mythological level. In fact John Short's moving poem is almost the only one I am aware of. I know little about its author except that he was born in 1911 and was the author of a single book, now apparently unobtainable, *The Oak and the Ash*, published by J. M. Dent.

Carol

by John Short

There was a Boy bedded in bracken
Like to a sleeping snake all curled he lay
On his thin navel turned this spinning sphere
Each feeble finger fetched seven suns away
He was not dropped in good-for-lambing weather
He took no suck when shook buds sing together
But he is come in cold-as-workhouse weather
Poor as a Salford child.

The reasons for the once enormous popularity of Dylan Thomas's work are now hard to comprehend. His poetry is certainly not overly 'accessible', even if it does not consist merely, as Kingsley Amis once said, of 'unanswerable riddles'. On the other hand it is certainly 'affirmative', which is always a help towards popularity. When it comes to the big questions of birth and death – and what a one he is for the big questions! – Dylan nearly always returns, or seems to return, an affirmative answer.

And there was of course the lifestyle of the man himself, which fitted the popular conception of 'the poet' to a nicety. The poet was lecherous, noisy, impecunious, untrustworthy and seemingly more often drunk than sober. As a sort of bonus Dylan was genuinely loveable and could be very funny about his misfortunes.

What more could one ask? Dylan – it was, as Dannie Abse once pointed out, impossible to call him Thomas – was promoted into astounding status and still more surprising popularity. But the reaction has been severe. Dylan's merits and successes are now just as likely to be overlooked as his phoniness and failings were in the 1950s. He wrote a handful of beautiful and sometimes profound lyrics which will long outlive anything his attackers in 'the Movement' wrote; and outlive also his own more prolix and manufactured efforts.

'In My Craft Or Sullen Art' is one of them. Of course it is not entirely 'true' – he almost certainly writes for other reasons than the one given. But it is true in mood; and it says true things, while being, as well, astonishingly apt in epithet – the 'raging moon' and the 'spindrift pages' would be hard to beat.

In My Craft Or Sullen Art

by Dylan Thomas

In my craft or sullen art
Exercised in the still night
When only the moon rages
And the lovers lie abed
With all their griefs in their arms,
I labour by singing light
Not for ambition or bread
Or the strut and trade of charms
On the ivory stages
But for the common wages
Of their most secret heart.

Not for the proud man apart
From the raging moon I write
On these spindrift pages
Nor for the towering dead
With their nightingales and psalms
But for the lovers, their arms
Round the griefs of the ages,
Who pay no praise or wages
Nor heed my craft or art.

Yeats's primary symbols of humanity were much the same as Shakespeare's: the king, the queen, the fool, the player or actor; but he added a clutch of his own: the beggar, the poet, the hermit and the Kevin O'Higgins-like hero of action. 'Beggar to Beggar Cried' comes from *Responsibilities*, published in 1914, in which there are two or three other fine beggar poems.

The idea of very beautiful women being difficult to deal with was one that he adverted to elsewhere — perhaps he thought he had good reason. One of his least remarked on characteristics as a poet is his humour. Maybe it escapes notice because so many of his admirers seem to be lacking in that very quality.

Beggar To Beggar Cried

by W. B. Yeats

'Time to put off the world and go somewhere
And find my health again in the sea air,'
Beggar to beggar cried, being frenzy-struck,
'And make my soul before my pate is bare.'

'And get a comfortable wife and house
To rid me of the devil in my shoes,'
Beggar to beggar cried being frenzy-struck,
'And the worse devil that is between my thighs.'

'And though I'd marry with a comely lass,
She need not be too comely – let it pass,'
Beggar to beggar cried, being frenzy-struck,
'But there's a devil in a looking-glass.'

'Nor should she be too rich, because the rich
Are driven by wealth as beggars by the itch,'
Beggar to beggar cried, being frenzy-struck,
'And cannot have a humorous happy speech.'

'And there I'll grow respected at my ease
And hear amid the garden's nightly peace,'
Beggar to beggar cried, being frenzy-struck,
'The wind-blown clamour of the barnacle geese.'

In spite of his unruffled Victorian exterior — the mutton chop whiskers and the high, winged collar — Matthew Arnold was a passionate and doughty fighter for a number of worthy causes (as well as a number of others hardly worth fighting for); and a stern critic of what he saw as the provinciality, Philistinism, narrow sectarianism and gross materialism of English life. He tried hard to maintain critical standards at a time when, as he saw it, they were being steadily undermined and destroyed.

In most of his battles and endeavours he was, needless to say, on the losing side, which is what this little poem is about.

The Last Word

by Matthew Arnold

Creep into thy narrow bed,
Creep, and let no more be said!
Vain thy onset! All stands fast.
Thou thyself must break at last.

Let the long contention cease!
Geese are swans, and swans are geese.
Let them have it how they will!
Thou art tired, best be still.

They out-talked thee, hissed thee, tore thee?
Better men fared thus before thee,
Fired their ringing shot and passed
Hotly charged – and sank at last.

Charge once more, then, and be dumb!
Let the victors, when they come,
When the forts of folly fall,
Find thy body by the wall!

In 1941 Auden wrote a sort of meditation on Shakespeare's play, *The Tempest*. In the play, Stephano finds a cask of wine which has been washed ashore and sings a song under its influence, which refers to Kate and Margery. Auden evidently adopted it as his starting point, but the song that he gives his drunken mariners is one of those astonishing lyrics that seem to sum up much of human life in a few melodic, tragi-comic lines.

The Mariner's Song

from *The Sea and The Mirror*

by W. H. Auden

At Dirty Dick's and Sloppy Joe's
We drank our liquor straight,
Some went upstairs with Margery,
And some, alas, with Kate;
And two by two like cat and mouse
The homeless played at keeping house.

There Wealthy Meg, the Sailor's Friend,
And Marion, cow-eyed,
Opened their arms to me but I
Refused to step inside;
I was not looking for a cage
In which to mope in my old age.

The nightingales are sobbing in
The orchards of our mothers,
And hearts that we broke long ago
Have long been breaking others;
Tears are round, the sea is deep:
Roll them overboard and sleep.

This wonderful quatrain is a song from *The Winter's Tale*, one of Shakespeare's late dramas of reconciliation (usually brought about through the agency of a beautiful daughter). C. H. Sisson has said that this and other such verses could not have been written if Shakespeare had not been steeped in the traditional anonymous versification of England — what we now call nursery rhymes; and suggested that he may even have called them out of memory 'with more or less variation'.

Song

by William Shakespeare

Jog on, jog on, the footpath way,
And merrily hent the stile-a:
A merry heart goes all the day,
Your sad one tires in a mile-a.

More than any other writer one can think of, Kipling has suffered for his lack of political correctness. Racist, anti-feminist, imperialist – the catalogue of his sins is long and has been many times listed by a certain type of critic.

Fortunately, though, he has had influential admirers who were not over-worried by such matters – 'the common reader' of course, first and foremost, but also T. S. Eliot, W. H. Auden, Berthold Brecht and, in his native India, Nirad Chaudhuri.

The truth is that, whatever his occasionally obnoxious views, Kipling was a poet, with all that implies in the way of self-contradiction and ultimate truth. His poetry is a perfect example of Auden's dictum that 'all kinds of poetry are good except the boring kind'.

Sometimes he was a great poet, going directly to the heart of things. 'Gertrude's Prayer' springs from his own unhappy childhood. We may regret the archaic diction – which incidentally demands that the words 'oake' and 'hour' be given two syllables – but if you read it a few times without troubling yourself too much about the meaning of certain words, you will see that it speaks for all misused and mishandled children; and that what it is saying is profoundly and terribly true. The title is accounted for by the fact that Kipling sometimes wrote poems as prefaces to short stories. This one was pre-fixed to a story in the volume *Limits and Renewals*.

Gertrude's Prayer

by Rudyard Kipling

That which is marred at birth Time shall not mend,
Nor water out of bitter well make clean;
All evil thing returneth at the end,
Or elseway walketh in our blood unseen.
Whereby the more is sorrow in certaine –
Dayspring mishandled cometh not againe.

To-bruized be that slender, sterting spray
Out of the oake's rind that should betide
A branch of girt and goodliness, straightway
Her spring is turned on herself, and wried
And knotted like some gall or veiny wen –
Dayspring mishandled cometh not agen.

Noontide repayeth never morning-bliss –
Sith noon to morn is incomparable;
And, so it be our dawning goeth amiss,
None other after hour serveth well.
Ah! Jesu-Moder, pitie my oe paine –
Dayspring mishandled cometh not againe.

The lament of the exiled poet, Deor, is one of the very earliest poems in the English or Anglo-Saxon language. Judging from the verse itself, he was a court poet who had been eclipsed by a rival. Each stanza refers to a story of misfortune which would have been well-known to his Anglo-Saxon audience. It may be exceedingly egotistical of him to compare his disappointment and loss of emolument with these famous epitomes of trouble and disaster, but it is surely because of this personal note that his poem speaks to us so immediately over the centuries. The version given here is of course a modernisation, in effect a translation, by Michael Alexander. 'Makar' was the old English word for poet; and a much better word too.

Deor

Wayland knew the wanderer's fate:
that single-willed earl suffered agonies,
sorrow and longing the sole companions
of his ice-cold exile. Anxieties bit
when Nithad put a knife to his hamstrings,
laid clever bonds on the better man.

That went by; this may too.

Beadohild mourned her murdered brothers:
but her own plight pained her more
— her womb grew great with child.
When she knew that, she could never hold
Steady before her wit what was to happen.

That went by; this may too.

We all know that Eormanric
had a wolf's wit. Wide Gothland
lay in the grasp of that grim king,
and through it many sat, by sorrows environed,
foreseeing only sorrow; sighed for the downfall
and thorough overthrow of the thrall-maker.

That went by; this may too.

Of myself in this regard I shall say this only:
that in the hall of the Heodenings I held long the makarship,
lived dear to my prince, Deor my name;

many winters I held this happy place
and my lord was kind. Then came Heorrenda,
whose lays were skilful; the lord of fighting-men
settled on him the estate bestowed once on me.

That went by; this may too.

Oliver Goldsmith does not bulk as large in the Irish consciousness now as he did when Foley's remarkable statue was erected outside Trinity. Part of the decline in Goldsmith's general reputation is, I think, attributable to nineteenth-century biography, which insisted on the 'gentle', 'whimsical', 'lovable' Goldsmith, whereas the real Goldsmith was a tippler and a compulsive gambler who preferred the company and the delights offered by 'ladies of the town' to more respectable society – in other words, a far more interesting fellow.

He had a busy and varied literary career but as a poet he would be largely forgotten now if, towards the end of it, he had not had the luck to write *The Deserted Village*. These are the closing lines, a noble and moving exordium to poetry itself. The prophecy in them has largely come true, for the muse has more or less deserted England, if not for 'Torno's Cliffs' and 'Pambamarca's side', at least as for other places where English is spoken and written.

from The Deserted Village

by Oliver Goldsmith

And thou, sweet Poetry, thou loveliest maid,
Still first to fly where sensual joys invade;
Unfit in these degenerate times of shame,
To catch the heart, or strike for honest fame;
Dear charming nymph, neglected and decried,
My shame in crowds, my solitary pride;
Thou source of all my bliss, and all my woe,
That found'st me poor at first, and keep'st me so;
Thou guide by which the nobler arts excel,
Thou nurse of every virtue, fare thee well.
Farewell, and O where'er thy voice be tried,
On Torno's cliffs, or Pambamraca's side,
Whether where equinoctial fervours glow,
Or winter wraps the polar world in snow,
Still let they voice prevailing over time,
Redress the rigours of the inclement clime;
Aid slighted truth, with thy persuasive strain
Teach erring man to spurn the rage of gain;
Teach him that states of native strength possesst,
Though very poor, may still be very blest;
That trade's proud empire hastes to swift decay,
As ocean sweeps the laboured mole away;
While self-dependent power can time defy,
As rocks resist the billows and the sky.

Grateful acknowledgement is made to the following for permission to reproduce copyrighted material.

Carcanet Press Limited, 4th Floor, Conavon Court, 12-16 Blackfriars Street, Manchester M3 5BQ, England: 'Poem for Margot Heinemann' by John Cornford, from *Collected Writings*; 'As You Were Saying' by David Wright from *To The Gods The Shades*; 'The Wind Suffers' by Laura Riding, from *Selected Poems*.

The Marvell Press, 5 Los Angeles Court, East St Kilda, Victoria 3138, Australia: 'Deceptions' by Philip Larkin, from *Collected Poems*.

Faber and Faber, 3 Queen Square, London WC1N 3AU, England: 'The Mariner's Song' by W. H. Auden, from *Collected Poems*; 'Lullaby' (Lay Your Sleeping Head) by W. H. Auden, from *Collected Poems*; 'Our Lady of Walshingham' by Robert Lowell, from *Robert Lowell's Poems: A Selection*; 'Thalassa' by Louis MacNeice, from *Collected Poems*.

The Literary Trustees of Walter De La Mare and the Society of Authors as their representative, 84 Drayton Gardens, London SW10 9SB, England: 'The Listeners' and 'The Song of the Mad Prince' by Walter De La Mare, from *The Complete Poems of Walter De La Mare* (Faber).

W. W. Norton & Company, 500 Fifth Avenue, New York, NY 10110-0017, USA: 'The Bridge' by Hart Crane from *Complete Poems of Hart Crane*, edited by Marc Simon.

Máire Colum O'Sullivan, Glandore, Stradbrook Road, Blackrock, Co Dublin: 'The Old Woman of the Roads' by Padraic Colum, from *Collected Poems* (Oxford University Press).

David Higham Associates, 5-8 Lower John Street, Golden Square, London W1R 4HA, England: 'In My Craft Or Sullen Art' by Dylan Thomas from *Collected Poems* (Dent).

John Murray, 50 Albemarle Street, London W1X 4 BD, England: 'Youth and Age on Beaulieu River, Hants' by John Betjeman from *Collected Poems*.

'Carol' by John Short, from *The Oak and the Ash*, published by J. M. Dent.